TRILOGY

Also by H. D.

Collected Poems, 1912–1944

End to Torment: A Memoir of Ezra Pound

The Gift

The Hedgehog

Helen in Egypt

Hermetic Definition

HERmione

Kora and Ka

Nights

Selected Poems

Tribute to Freud

TRILOGY

The Walls Do Not Fall

Tribute to the Angels

The Flowering of the Rod

by H.D.

Introduction and Readers' Notes

by Aliki Barnstone

A New Directions Book

Some of the poems included in this collection also appeared in *Selected Poems,* published by Grove Press Inc., New York, 1957.

First published clothbound and as New Directions Paperbook 362 in 1973.
Reissued in 1998 as New Directions Paperbook 866.

Manufactured in the United States of America
New Directions Books are printed on acid-free paper.
Published simultaneously in Canada by Penguin Books Canada Limited.

Library of Congress Cataloging-in-Publication Data

H. D. (Hilda Doolittle), 1886–1961
Trilogy / by H. D. ; Introduction and notes by Aliki Barnstone.
p. cm.
Contents: The walls do not fall—Tribute to the angels—The flowering of the rod.
ISBN 978-0-8112-1399-8
I. Barnstone, Aliki. II. Title
PS3507.0726T74 1998 98-22882
811'.52—dc21 CIP

New Directions Books are published for James Laughlin
by New Directions Corporation
80 Eighth Avenue, New York 10011

EIGHTH PRINTING

CONTENTS

INTRODUCTION

In *Tribute to Freud,* H.D. asks, "Do I wish myself, in the deepest unconscious or subconscious layers of my being, to be the founder of a new religion?" *Trilogy* is H.D.'s complex answer to this question. If with this astonishing book of poetry H.D. does not establish a new religion, she certainly "makes it new" while creating an eclectic scripture that derives from Egyptian, Greek, and biblical traditions. Despite her enormous output and radical poetics, H.D.'s reputation lingers unfairly back in the early decades of the century, under the restrictive label of "Imagist," one which she adamently rejected. *Trilogy,* however, (1944) establishes her as a major poet among the other modernists—a large-minded and philosophical visionary. Like T.S. Eliot's *The Waste Land,* William Carlos Williams' *Paterson,* and Ezra Pound's *Cantos, Trilogy* is an epic poem that takes the reader on the poet's political, spiritual, philosophical, and artistic quest. Each poet, like their precursors Milton, Whitman, and Baudelaire, has composed a personal bible; *Trilogy* is H.D.'s multilayered sacred text.

In comparing *Trilogy* to her earlier work, H.D. wrote: "This is not the 'crystalline' poetry that my early critics would insist on. It is no pillar of salt nor yet of hewn rock-crystal. It is the pillar of fire by night, the pillar of cloud by day."[1] She refers to the story of the children of Israel escaping Egypt in Exodus 13.21: "And the Lord went before them by day in a pillar of a cloud, to lead them the way; and by night in a pillar of fire, to give them light; to go by day and night." Her poem, she implies, is an incarnation of God's

[1] Quoted in Susan Stanford Friedman, *Psyche Reborn: The Emergence of H.D.* (Bloomington: Indiana UP, 1981), p. 8.

words, showing the path. She asks the reader to venerate both her voice and the figure of Woman as poet, mystical seer, and god.

H.D. wrote *Trilogy* during World War II. She had not left London during the German bombing of the city. "The orgy of destructions . . . to be witnessed and lived through in London, that outer threat and constant reminder of death," she wrote, "drove me inward" (NHP, v).[2] So *The Walls Do Not Fall* begins with

> An incident [bombing] here and there,
> and rails gone (for guns)
> from your (and my) old town square.

In a letter to Norman Holmes Pearson, she reflects upon her comparison of London to Egypt in the first section of *Walls;* the ruins of both places expose the relics of our unconscious worlds:

> The parallel between ancient Egypt and 'ancient' London is obvious. In [section] I the 'fallen roof leaves the sealed room open to the air' is of course true of our own house of life—outer violence touching the deepest hidden subconscious terrors, etc., and we see so much of our past 'on show', as it were 'another sliced wall where poor utensils show like rare objects in a museum'. Egypt? London? Mystery, majic—that I have found in London! (NHP, vii).

H.D. read the mystery in the signs—or the hieroglyphs left in the ruins—"two ways," as she might say: as terror and as magic. Out of the "orgy of destructions" which "drove her inward," she wrote a book of hope, a book of life, and a scripture for a new religion. *Trilogy* asserts the power of the word over the sword, for "without idea and the Word's mediation, // [the sword] would have remained / unmanifest." While the German planes roared overhead, bombs falling, she heard a more powerful voice, which she calls "Dream / Vision":

[2] NHP is the abbreviation for Norman Holmes Pearson's foreword to the first New Direcctions edition of *Trilogy*.

though there was whirr and roar in the high air
there was a Voice louder.

Trilogy synthesizes the Judeo-Christian tradition (including Gnosticism) with the Egyptian and Greek pagan traditions. H.D.'s book reveals that the gods, goddesses, and the figures in the Bible are

the same—different—the same attributes,
different yet the same as before.

She brings together the old and the new, the scientific and pragmatic, and the esoteric and mystical. The differences between people—especially their religious differences—ignite war. *Trilogy* shows that differences are also similarities or affinities that, with enlightenment, can ignite love rather than war, creation rather than destruction—and resurrection out of Apocalypse:

chasm, schism in consciousness
must be bridged over;

we are each, householder,
each with a treasure

Love, which brings difference together in harmony, is the answer: "only love is holy." Jesus Christ is the divine embodiment of love; so too and with equal importance is the woman god: Isis, Astarte, Aphrodite, Venus, Mary, The Lady.

As the poem itself points out, *Trilogy* is a "palimpsest," in which one might see the old writing under the new, beneath layers of transparencies. This quality of being "different yet the same as before" intentionally mimics the typological structure of the Bible, which is itself a palimpsest of pre-biblical legends. The New Testament gospels are reworkings of Old Testament texts and of each other. H.D. writes:

In no wise is the pillar-of-fire
that went before

different from the pillar-of-fire
that comes after . . .

Here, she refers to the pillars-of-fire in both the Old and New Testaments. The old pillar-of-fire is the light given Moses and the children of Israel by the Lord at night as they escape from Egypt; the new is the angel of Revelation whose feet are pillars-of-fire. H.D. bridges the "schism in consciousness" by revealing that the light of God is always the light of God, whether it is ancient Egyptian or Greek, Old or New Testament, male or female.

Trilogy is also deeply informed by H.D.'s work as an analysand with Sigmund Freud[3] She calls him "this old Janus, this beloved light-house keeper, old Captain January."[4] Janus was the God who faced two ways and was the guardian of doorways and roads. Freud was guardian of the doorway between the conscious and unconscious minds. H.D.'s book, *Tribute to Freud,* is indeed a tribute to the man who revolutionized the way human consciousness is understood. It is also a guide to H.D.'s own philosophy and poetics, as can be seen in her interpretation of Freud's philosophy of dreams:

> He had said, he had dared to say that the dream had its worth and value in translatable terms, not the dream merely of a Pharaoh or a Pharaoh's butler, not the dream merely of the favorite child of Israel, not merely Joseph's dream or Jacob's dream of a symbolic ladder, not the dream only of the Cumaean Sybil of Italy or the Delphic Priestess of ancient Greece, but the dream of everyone, everywhere. He had dared to say that the dream came from an unexplored depth in man's consciousness and that this unexplored depth ran like a great stream or ocean underground, and the vast depth of that ocean was the same vast depth that today, as in Joseph's day, overflowing in man's small consciousness, pro-

[3] For extensive analysis of H.D. and Freud, see Susan Friedman, Diane Chisholm, *H.D.'s Freudian Poetics: Psychoanalysis in Translation* (Ithaca: Cornell University Press, 1992), and Clare Buck, *H.D. & Freud: Bisexuality and a Feminine Discourse* (New York: St Martin's Press, 1991).

[4] *Tribute to Freud* (New York: New Directions, 1956), p. 102.

> duced inspiration, madness, creative idea, or the dregs of the dreariest symptoms of mental unrest and disease. He had dared to say that it was the same ocean of universal consciousness, and even if not stated in so many words, he had dared to imply that this consciousness proclaimed all men one; all nations and races met in the universal world of the dream; and he had dared to say that the dream-symbol could be interpreted; its language, its imagery were common to the whole race, not only of the living but of those ten thousand years dead. The picture-writing, the hieroglyph of the dream, was the common property of the whole race; in the dream, man, as at the beginning of time, spoke a universal language, and man, meeting in the universal understanding of the unconscious or the subconscious, would forgo barriers of time and space, and man, understanding man, would save mankind. (TF, 71)

In her elegantly passionate distillation of Freud, she reveals her absorption in his theories as well as her own departures from them. She incorporates Freud's ideas into her philosophy, yet she does so on her own terms: "But there was an argument implicit in our very bones." For all her admiration for his prophetic discoveries, H.D. asserts: "I was a student, working under the direction of the greatest mind of this and perhaps many succeeding generations. But the Professor was not always right" (TF, 18). The "hieroglyph of the dream" includes religious figures, both biblical and pagan. For Freud these are figures revealed through empirical psychological methods, whose significance is not transcendental but scientific: "[He} shut the door on transcendental speculations or at least transferred this occult or hidden symbolism to the occult or hidden regions of personal reactions, dreams. . . . It was the human individual that concerned him, its individual reactions to the problems of every-day" (TF, 102). Freud was concerned with bringing up the materials of the unconscious so that the individual could live rationally, not driven by the destructive forces of the unconscious. In contrast, H.D. ruminates on "what happened when this life was over" (TF, 102). She believes that the hieroglyph of the dream translates into otherworldly, spiritual signs. The dream is as Emerson, her philosophical soul-mate, puts it: "a temple whose walls are covered with emblems, pictures and commandments of the Deity."[5]

In 1920 on the island of Corfu in Greece, on the wall of her hotel room, H.D. saw a vision, which she calls the writing-on-the-wall. She notes: "There had been writing-on-walls before, in Biblical, in classic literature. At least, all through time, there had been a tradition of warnings or messages from another world or another state of being" (TF, 50). H.D. refers here to the biblical story of the prophet Daniel who interpreted King Belshazzar's vision of a hand writing on a wall. The writing prophesied disaster, for it said, "God hath numbered thy kingdom, and finished it. . . . In that night was Belshazzar the king of the Chaldean slain" (Daniel 5.25 & 30). On one level, H.D.'s writing-on-the-wall foretold the threat of the Germans starting World War II. On another, it is a religious vision, a kind of hope or answer that provides the material of her own luminous poetry.

Freud reads H.D.'s vision on the wall as "megalomania . . . a hidden desire to 'found a new religion'. . . . 'a dangerous symptom'" (TF, 51). H.D. responds that regardless of the label, "symptom or inspiration, the writing continues to write itself or be written" (TF, 51). H.D. has a holistic vision in which poetry, especially her own prophetic poetry, "can be translated into terms of today . . . common to the whole race" (TF, 51). She observes that religion, art, and medicine have become increasingly separated and she imagines:

> These three working together, to form a new vehicle of expression or new form of thing or of living, might be symbolized by the tripod. . . . The tripod . . . was the symbol of prophesy . . . the Priestess of Pythoness of Delphi sat on the tripod while she pronounced her verse couplets, the famous

[5] Ralph Waldo Emerson, "The Poet" in *Complete Writings* (New York: Wm. H. Wise, 1929), p. 243. Significantly, both Emerson and H.D. use the lexicon of John's Revelation. See *Tribute to the Angels*, p. 64.

Delphic utterances which it was said could be read two ways. (TF, 51)

In *Trilogy* H.D. synthesizes the three disciplines of religion, art, and medicine, figuring herself as the Priestess and as the scribe.

As a poet she identifies with the Egyptian Thoth and the Alexandrian Hermes Trismegistes, the mystical scribes, messengers, and healers. She remarks that dreams "are healing. They are real" (TF, 35). Likewise, in *Trilogy* she puts forth the imperative to "rededicate our gifts / to spiritual realism" and to pay homage to the Thoth/Hermes, who will "lead us back to the one-truth." She instructs us to prepare our writing tools and transcribe:

scrape a palette,
point pen or brush,

prepare papyrus or parchment,
offer incense to Thoth,

the original Ancient-of-days,
Hermes-thrice-great.

As the scribe or transcriber of the writing-on-the-wall, or the hieroglyph of the dream, the poet has special sight. H.D. wishes through her "spiritual realism" to show that those who claim that "poets are useless" are wrong. Poets speak a universal language that is the hope of humanity.

In keeping with her belief that Freud's reading of the unconscious "would save mankind," H.D. compared him to the other savior, Jesus: "There was another Jew who said, *the kingdom of heaven is within you*" (TF, 104). In *Trilogy* H.D. creates a poetics combining the salvific forces of Freud and Jesus Christ. A recurrent trope of the book is that it is "a tale of a Fisherman," a biblical reference which can be found in the gospels: "Now as he walked by the sea of Galilee, he saw Simon and Andrew his brother casting a net into the sea: for they were fishers. And Jesus said unto them, Come ye after me, and I will make you to become fishers of men" (Mk 1.16-17). Jesus says that Simon and Andrew will draw to them human souls; similarly, H.D. sees Freud as a fisher of human souls because by exploring the ocean of the unconscious, he discovers the "pearl-of-great-price":

the shark-jaws
of outer circumstance

will spit you forth:
be indigestible, hard, ungiving,

so that, living within,
you beget, self-out-of-self,

selfless,
that pearl-of-great-price.

In a Freudian context, the "pearl-of-great-price" is the self which "living within" is protected from "outer circumstance." Yet the pearl-of-great-price is from one of Jesus's parables in which a merchant sells all he has to buy it. The kingdom of heaven is like a net cast into the sea which, "when it was full, they drew to shore, and sat down, and gathered the good into vessels, but cast the bad away. So shall it be at the end of the world: the angels shall come forth, and sever the wicked from among the just" (Matthew 13.45–49). There is a cosmic difference between the inner worlds of Freud and H.D.: for H.D., the pearl-of-great-price is not the Freudian secular self, but the self which, by journeying within and shunning the evils of "outer circumstance," finds within the soul "the kingdom of heaven."

If H.D. incorporates Freud into her work on her own terms, she also does so with Jesus. Jesus is just one among the prophets, visionaries, and gods who populate *Trilogy's* pantheon. The poet wishes to "re-light the flame" of womanly vision and of the goddesses. Like Janus, "Gods always face two ways," toward the past and the future. So in *Trilogy* the Virgin Mary faces the past, becoming Isis, Astarte, Aphrodite, Venus, and she faces the future, immortalized as *the Lady* of H.D.'s vision. H.D. draws a connection between the denigration of the goddesses as "harlots" and "old flesh-pots" and the disparagement of women writers. She has high ambitions for poetry as a universal healing and regenerative force. The exclusion of women from the spirit or the word implies a terrible "schism in consciousness," to use her words.

In *Tribute to the Angels* the speaker has a vision of the Lady, who is a synthesis of all the holy women who have been portrayed in art, and all the goddesses, including Eve and Mary. "She carries a book" and, in these Gnostic lines, she redeems the feminine aspect of the soul and Eve:

> Ah (you say), this is Holy Wisdom,
> *Santa Sophia,* the SS of the *Sanctus Spiritus,*
>
> so by facile reasoning, logically
> the incarnate symbol of the Holy Ghost;
>
> your Holy Ghost was an apple-tree
> smouldering—or rather now bourgeoning
>
> with flowers; the fruit of the Tree?
> this is the new Eve who comes
>
> clearly to return, to retrieve
> what she lost the race,
>
> given over to sin, to death;
> she brings the Book of Life, obviously.

This poem combines Gnosticism with H.D.'s Moravian background in order to redeem Eve for her sinless knowledge and independence—and to redeem women since they are blamed for Eve's "sin." Historically, the Moravian church, in which H.D. was raised, exalted the feminine. Count Zinzendorf, the founder of the Moravian Church, was denounced as a heretic for claiming that the human soul was female, *anima* rather than *animus,* and connecting the soul with *Sophia,* the female *Holy Spirit* of Gnosticism. Susan Friedman explains: "Many Moravians were burned for witchcraft, but they continued to worship secretly with a cup decorated with an 'S.' This 'S' did not represent the serpent of the Devil, but an earlier serpent symbol that signified the 'Sanctus Spiritus, the Holy Spirit.'"[6]

[6] Friedman, p. 183.

In the writing-on-the-wall, H.D. saw these Moravian and Gnostic symbols: "The *S* or half-*S* faces the angel; that is, the series of the *S*-pattern opens out in the direction of the angel; they are like question marks . . . this inverted *S*-pattern may have represented a series of question marks, the questions that have been asked through the ages, that the ages will go on asking" (TF, 55). These eternal questions are Gnostic (which means one who knows), since they point to a quest for knowledge. The S of the serpent is also Gnostic, since the serpent is holy, urging Eve to seek knowledge. Eve is a savior because she gave knowledge, the fruit of the Tree, to humanity. The traditional Eve of the Bible lost immortality and respect and veneration. In H.D.'s revision "the new Eve . . . comes / clearly to retrieve / what she lost." The new Eve has transformed her punishment. No longer "given over to sin, to death; / she brings the Book of Life, obviously." The burned-out apple tree, a recurrent motif in *Trilogy*, is "now bourgeoning / with flowers." And the flowers are the flowers of rebirth, resurrection, and immortality which grow from Eve's knowledge and, it is implied, from the Tree of the Knowledge of Good and Evil.

Eve's "Book of Life" appears two sections later, transformed into possibility, hope for freedom, and beauty, and the future:

> she carries a book but it is not
> the tome of the ancient wisdom,
>
> the pages, I imagine, are the blank pages
> of the unwritten volume of the new;
>
> all you say, is implicit,
> all that and much more;
>
> but she is not shut up in a cave
> like a Sibyl; she is not
>
> imprisoned in leaden bars
> in a coloured window;
>
> she is Psyche, the butterfly,
> out of the cocoon.

The Lady is not "imprisoned in leaden bars / in a coloured window." That is, she is not the Lady portrayed by the stained glass in church, nor is she limited to the objectification and trap of artistic images. She is unlike the Sybil caught for centuries in a cave, who, despite her prophetic knowledge, wishes to die rather than to live. The Lady has advanced beyond "the tome of ancient wisdom," for the pages of her book are the pages of new creations: "the pages, I imagine, are the blank pages / of the unwritten volume of the new." H.D., as all writers must do to make their words live, invites her reader to recreate the text of *Trilogy*. (Without a reader, a text is merely an object with no consciousness, no *anima.*) The Word of poetry is regenerative; *Trilogy* is not a closed text, written for itself, but one that opens up the Book of Life, and shows the reader the blank pages on which she or he can write "the new." When the Lady becomes "Psyche, the butterfly, / out of the cocoon," the spirit is free to fly, displaying, creating, and recreating the beauty of the soul. Open *Trilogy* and you will see, rising from between the ink and the blank spaces in the pages, H.D.'s Psyche, her butterfly.

* * *

This project grew directly from my teaching *Trilogy*. I discovered that without an understanding of H.D.'s references, students found *Trilogy* too elusive and mystifying to appreciate. I asked them to look up her references and make glossaries. The result was a turnaround. With the power of knowledge my students experienced the exhilaration of engaging with this philosophically complex and difficult text.

In my annotations, I have tried to be informative, not interpretive, though I acknowledge that the annotations themselves are a form of interpretation. Since H.D. weaves into her text an encyclopedic knowledge of the occult, mythology, esoteric religion, Gnosticism, and the Bible, the task of annotating *Trilogy* is probably limitless. My goal has been not to provide a gloss for each line of the poem, but to illuminate the most important allusions. Annotating *Trilogy* has taught me that seeking the sources is part of the reading experience of the book. By sending her readers to other works,

H.D. sends them on an intertextual journey that helps them recreate the text, and, in some measure, her own creative process. I would like to suggest, however, that you read *Trilogy* once without consulting the notes, then read again allowing the notes to inform your own intuitive response.

My hope is that this annotation will make *Trilogy* more accessible to readers, and that teachers will be encouraged to have the heady experience of teaching one of the stunning poems of the century.

I wish to thank Willis Barnstone, Kathleen Crown, Shannon Doyne, and Elizabeth Sahm-Kelly for their invaluable assistance. And I owe special gratitude to Perdita Schaffner for permitting me voyage.

Aliki Barnstone
Lewisburg, Pennsylvania
March 1998

THE WALLS DO NOT FALL

To Bryher

for Karnak 1923
from London 1942

[1]

An incident here and there,
and rails gone (for guns)
from your (and my) old town square:

mist and mist-grey, no colour,
still the Luxor bee, chick and hare
pursue unalterable purpose

in green, rose-red, lapis;
they continue to prophesy
from the stone papyrus:

there, as here, ruin opens
the tomb, the temple; enter,
there as here, there are no doors:

the shrine lies open to the sky,
the rain falls, here, there
sand drifts; eternity endures:

ruin everywhere, yet as the fallen roof
leaves the sealed room
open to the air,

so, through our desolation,
thoughts stir, inspiration stalks us
through gloom:

unaware, Spirit announces the Presence;
shivering overtakes us,
as of old, Samuel:

trembling at a known street-corner,
we know not nor are known;
the Pythian pronounces—we pass on

to another cellar, to another sliced wall
where poor utensils show
like rare objects in a museum;

Pompeii has nothing to teach us,
we know crack of volcanic fissure,
slow flow of terrible lava,

pressure on heart, lungs, the brain
about to burst its brittle case
(what the skull can endure!):

over us, Apocryphal fire,
under us, the earth sway, dip of a floor,
slope of a pavement

where men roll, drunk
with a new bewilderment,
sorcery, bedevilment:

the bone-frame was made for
no such shock knit within terror,
yet the skeleton stood up to it:

the flesh? it was melted away,
the heart burnt out, dead ember,
tendons, muscles shattered, outer husk dismembered,

yet the frame held:
we passed the flame: we wonder
what saved us? what for?

[2]

Evil was active in the land,
Good was impoverished and sad;

Ill promised adventure,
Good was smug and fat;

Dev-ill was after us,
tricked up like Jehovah;

Good was the tasteless pod,
stripped from the manna-beans, pulse, lentils:

they were angry when we were so hungry
for the nourishment, God;

they snatched off our amulets,
charms are not, they said, grace;

but gods always face two-ways,
so let us search the old highways

for the true-rune, the right-spell,
recover old values;

nor listen if they shout out,
your beauty, Isis, Aset or Astarte,

is a harlot; you are retrogressive,
zealot, hankering after old flesh-pots;

your heart, moreover,
is a dead canker,

they continue, and
your rhythm is the devil's hymn,

your stylus is dipped in corrosive sublimate,
how can you scratch out

indelible ink of the palimpsest
of past misadventure?

[3]

Let us, however, recover the Sceptre,
the rod of power:

it is crowned with the lily-head
or the lily-bud:

it is Caduceus; among the dying
it bears healing:

or evoking the dead,
it brings life to the living.

[4]

There is a spell, for instance,
in every sea-shell:

continuous, the sea thrust
is powerless against coral,

bone, stone, marble
hewn from within by that craftsman,

the shell-fish:
oyster, clam, mollusc

is master-mason planning
the stone marvel:

yet that flabby, amorphous hermit
within, like the planet

senses the finite,
it limits its orbit

of being, its house,
temple, fane, shrine:

it unlocks the portals
at stated intervals:

prompted by hunger,
it opens to the tide-flow:

but infinity? no,
of nothing-too-much:

[7]

Gods, goddesses
wear the winged head-dress

of horns, as the butterfly
antennae,

or the erect king-cobra crest
to show how the worm turns.

[8]

So we reveal our status
with twin-horns, disk, erect serpent,

though these or the double-plume or lotus
are, you now tell us, trivial

intellectual adornment;
poets are useless,

more than that,
we, authentic relic,

bearers of the secret wisdom,
living remnant

of the inner band
of the sanctuaries' initiate,

are not only 'non-utilitarian',
we are 'pathetic':

this is the new heresy;
but if you do not even understand what words say,

how can you expect to pass judgement
on what words conceal?

yet the ancient rubrics reveal that
we are back at the beginning:

you have a long way to go,
walk carefully, speak politely

to those who have done their worm-cycle,
for gods have been smashed before

and idols and their secret is stored
in man's very speech,

in the trivial or
the real dream; insignia

in the heron's crest,
the asp's back,

enigmas, rubrics promise as before,
protection for the scribe;

he takes precedence of the priest,
stands second only to the Pharoah.

[9]

Thoth, Hermes, the stylus,
the palette, the pen, the quill endure,

though our books are a floor
of smouldering ash under our feet;

though the burning of the books remains
the most perverse gesture

and the meanest
of man's mean nature,

yet give us, they still cry,
give us books,

folio, manuscript, old parchment
will do for cartridge cases;

irony is bitter truth
wrapped up in a little joke,

and Hatshepsut's name is still circled
with what they call the *cartouche*.

[10]

But we fight for life,
we fight, they say, for breath,

so what good are your scribblings?
this—we take them with us

beyond death; Mercury, Hermes, Thoth
invented the script, letters, palette;

the indicated flute or lyre-notes
on papyrus or parchment

are magic, indelibly stamped
on the atmosphere somewhere,

forever; remember, O Sword,
you are the younger brother, the latter-born,

your Triumph, however exultant,
must one day be over,

in the beginning
was the Word.

[11]

Without thought, invention,
you would not have been, O Sword,

without idea and the Word's mediation,
you would have remained

unmanifest in the dim dimension
where thought dwells,

and beyond thought and idea,
their begetter,

Dream,
Vision.

[12]

So, in our secretive, sly way,
we are proud and chary

of companionship with you others,
our betters, who seem to imply

that we will soon be swept aside,
crumpled rags, no good for banner-stuff,

no fit length for a bandage;
but when the shingles hissed

in the rain of incendiary,
other values were revealed to us,

other standards hallowed us;
strange texture, a wing covered us,

and though there was whirr and roar in the high air,
there was a Voice louder,

though its speech was lower
than a whisper.

[13]

The Presence was spectrum-blue,
ultimate blue ray,

rare as radium, as healing;
my old self, wrapped round me,

was shroud (I speak of myself individually
but I was surrounded by companions

in this mystery);
do you wonder we are proud,

aloof,
indifferent to your good and evil?

peril, strangely encountered, strangely endured,
marks us;

we know each other
by secret symbols,

though, remote, speechless,
we pass each other on the pavement,

at the turn of the stair;
though no word pass between us,

there is subtle appraisement;
even if we snarl a brief greeting

or do not speak at all,
we know our Name,

we nameless initiates,
born of one mother,

companions
of the flame.

[14]

Yet we, the latter-day twice-born,
have our bad moments when

dragging the forlorn
husk of self after us,

we are forced to confess to
malaise and embarrassment;

we pull at this dead shell,
struggle but we must wait

till the new Sun dries off
the old-body humours;

awkwardly, we drag this stale
old will, old volition, old habit

about with us;
we are these people,

wistful, ironical, wilful,
who have no part in

new-world reconstruction,
in the confederacy of labour,

the practical issues of art
and the cataloguing of utilities:

O, do not look up
into the air,

you who are occupied
in the bewildering

sand-heap maze
of present-day endeavour;

you will be, not so much frightened
as paralysed with inaction,

and anyhow,
we have not crawled so very far

up our individual grass-blade
toward our individual star.

[15]

Too old to be useful
(whether in years or experience,

we are the same lot)
not old enough to be dead,

we are the keepers of the secret,
the carriers, the spinners

of the rare intangible thread
that binds all humanity

to ancient wisdom,
to antiquity;

our joy is unique, to us,
grape, knife, cup, wheat

are symbols in eternity,
and every concrete object

has abstract value, is timeless
in the dream parallel

whose relative sigil has not changed
since Nineveh and Babel.

[16]

Ra, Osiris, *Amen* appeared
in a spacious, bare meeting-house;

he is the world-father,
father of past aeons,

present and future equally;
beardless, not at all like Jehovah,

he was upright, slender,
impressive as the Memnon monolith,

yet he was not out of place
but perfectly at home

in that eighteenth-century
simplicity and grace;

then I woke with a start
of wonder and asked myself,

but whose eyes are those eyes?
for the eyes (in the cold,

I marvel to remember)
were all one texture,

as if without pupil
or all pupil, dark

yet very clear with amber
shining . . .

[17]

. . . coals for the world's burning,
for we must go forward,

we are at the cross-roads,
the tide is turning;

it uncovers pebbles and shells,
beautiful yet static, empty

old thought, old convention;
let us go down to the sea,

gather dry sea-weed,
heap drift-wood,

let us light a new fire
and in the fragrance

of burnt salt and sea-incense
chant new paeans to the new Sun

of regeneration;
we have always worshipped Him,

we have always said,
forever and ever, Amen.

[18]

The Christos-image
is most difficult to disentangle

from its art-craft junk-shop
paint-and-plaster medieval jumble

of pain-worship and death-symbol,
that is why, I suppose, the Dream

deftly stage-managed the bare, clean
early colonial interior,

without stained-glass, picture,
image or colour,

for now it appears obvious
that *Amen* is our Christos.

[19]

He might even be the authentic Jew
stepped out from Velasquez;

those eye-lids in the Velasquez
are lowered over eyes

that open, would daze, bewilder
and stun us with the old sense of guilt

and fear, but the terror of those eyes
veiled in their agony is over;

I assure you that the eyes
of Velasquez' crucified

now look straight at you,
and they are amber and they are fire.

[20]

Now it appears very clear
that the Holy Ghost,

childhood's mysterious enigma,
is the Dream;

that way of inspiration
is always open,

and open to everyone;
it acts as go-between, interpreter,

it explains symbols of the past
in to-day's imagery,

it merges the distant future
with most distant antiquity,

states economically
in a simple dream-equation

the most profound philosophy,
discloses the alchemist's secret

and follows the Mage
in the desert.

[21]

Splintered the crystal of identity,
shattered the vessel of integrity,

till the Lord *Amen*,
paw-er of the ground,

bearer of the curled horns,
bellows from the horizon:

here am I, Amen-Ra,
Amen, Aries, the Ram;

time, time for you to begin a new spiral,
see—I toss you into the star-whirlpool;

till pitying, pitying,
snuffing the ground,

here am I, Amen-Ra whispers,
Amen, Aries, the Ram,

be cocoon, smothered in wool,
be Lamb, mothered again.

[22]

Now my right hand,
now my left hand

clutch your curled fleece;
take me home, take me home,

my voice wails from the ground;
take me home, Father:

pale as the worm in the grass,
yet I am a spark

struck by your hoof from a rock:
Amen, you are so warm,

hide me in your fleece,
crop me up with the new-grass;

let your teeth devour me,
let me be warm in your belly,

the sun-disk,
the re-born Sun.

[23]

Take me home
where canals

flow
between iris-banks:

where the heron
has her nest:

where the mantis
prays on the river-reed:

where the grasshopper says
Amen, Amen, Amen.

[24]

Or anywhere
where stars blaze through clear air,

where we may greet individually,
Sirius, Vega, Arcturus,

where these separate entities
are intimately concerned with us,

where each, with its particular attribute,
may be invoked

with accurate charm, spell, prayer,
which will reveal unquestionably,

whatever healing or inspirational essence
is necessary for whatever particular ill

the inquiring soul is heir to:
O stars, little jars of that indisputable

and absolute Healer, Apothecary,
wrought, faceted, jewelled

boxes, very precious, to hold further
unguent, myrrh, incense:

jasper, beryl, sapphire
that, as we draw them nearer

by prayer, spell,
litany, incantation,

will reveal their individual fragrance,
personal magnetic influence,

become, as they once were,
personified messengers,

healers, helpers
of the One, *Amen*, All-father.

[25]

Amen,
only just now,

my heart-shell
breaks open,

though long ago, the phoenix,
your *bennu* bird

dropped a grain,
as of scalding wax;

there was fragrance, burnt incense,
myrtle, aloes, cedar;

the Kingdom is a Tree
whose roots bind the heart-husk

to earth,
after the ultimate grain,

lodged in the heart-core,
has taken its nourishment.

[26]

What fruit is our store,
what flower?

what savour do we possess,
what particular healing-of-the-nations

is our leaf? is it balsomodendron,
herb-basil, or is ours

the spear and leaf-spire
of the palm?

are we born from island or oasis
or do we stand

fruit-less on the field-edge,
to spread

shade to the wheat-gatherers
in the noon-heat?

[27]

Is ours lotus-tree
from the lotus-grove,

magnolia's heavy, heady, sleepy
dream?

or pomegranate
whose name decorates sonnets,

but either acid or over-ripe,
perfect only for the moment?

of all the flowering of the wood,
are we wild-almond, winter-cherry?

or are we pine or fir,
sentinel, solitary?

or cypress,
arbutus-fragrant?

[28]

O Heart, small urn
of porphyry, agate or cornelian,

how imperceptibly the grain fell
between a heart-beat of pleasure

and a heart-beat of pain;
I do not know how it came

nor how long it had lain there,
nor can I say

how it escaped tempest
of passion and malice,

nor why it was not washed away
in flood of sorrow,

or dried up in the bleak drought
of bitter thought.

[29]

Grant us strength to endure
a little longer,

now the heart's alabaster
is broken;

we would feed forever
on the amber honey-comb

of your remembered greeting,
but the old-self,

still half at-home in the world,
cries out in anger,

I am hungry, the children cry for food
and flaming stones fall on them;

our awareness leaves us defenceless;
O, for your Presence

among the fishing-nets
by the beached boats on the lake-edge;

when, in the drift of wood-smoke,
will you say again, as you said,

the baked fish is ready,
here is the bread?

[30]

I heard Scorpion whet his knife,
I feared Archer (taut his bow),

Goat's horns were threat,
would climb high? then fall low;

across the abyss
the Waterman waited,

this is the age of the new dimension,
dare, seek, seek further, dare more,

here is the alchemist's key,
it unlocks secret doors,

the present goes a step further
toward fine distillation of emotion,

the elixir of life, the philosopher's stone
is yours if you surrender

sterile logic, trivial reason;
so mind dispersed, dared occult lore,

found secret doors unlocked,
floundered, was lost in sea-depth,

sub-conscious ocean where Fish
move two-ways, devour;

when identity in the depth,
would merge with the best,

octopus or shark rise
from the sea-floor:

illusion, reversion of old values,
oneness lost, madness.

[31]

Wistfulness, exaltation,
a pure core of burning cerebration,

jottings on a margin,
indecipherable palimpsest scribbled over

with too many contradictory emotions,
search for finite definition

of the infinite, stumbling toward
vague cosmic expression,

obvious sentiment,
folder round a spiritual bank-account,

with credit-loss too starkly indicated,
a riot of unpruned imagination,

jottings of psychic numerical equations,
runes, superstitions, evasions,

invasion of the over-soul into a cup
too brittle, a jar too circumscribed,

a little too porous to contain the out-flowing
of water-about-to-be-changed-to-wine

at the wedding; barren search,
arrogance, over-confidence, pitiful reticence,

boasting, intrusion of strained
inappropriate allusion,

illusion of lost-gods, daemons;
gambler with eternity,

initiate of the secret wisdom,
bride of the kingdom,

reversion of old values,
oneness lost, madness.

[32]

Depth of the sub-conscious spews forth
too many incongruent monsters

and fixed indigestible matter
such as shell, pearl; imagery

done to death; perilous ascent,
ridiculous descent; rhyme, jingle,

overworked assonance, nonsense,
juxtaposition of words for words' sake,

without meaning, undefined; imposition,
deception, indecisive weather-vane;

disagreeable, inconsequent syllables,
too malleable, too brittle,

over-sensitive, under-definitive,
clash of opposites, fight of emotion

and sterile invention—
you find all this?

conditioned to the discrimination
of the colours of the lunar rainbow

and the outer layers of the feathers
of the butterfly's antennae,

we were caught up by the tornado
and deposited on no pleasant ground,

but we found the angle of incidence
equals the angle of reflection;

separated from the wandering stars
and the habits of the lordly fixed ones,

we noted that even the erratic burnt-out comet
has its peculiar orbit.

[33]

Let us measure defeat
in terms of bread and meat,

and continents
in relative extent of wheat

fields; let us not teach
what we have learned badly

and not profited by;
let us not concoct

healing potions for the dead,
nor invent

new colours
for blind eyes.

[34]

We have seen how the most amiable,
under physical stress,

become wolves, jackals,
mongrel curs;

we know further that hunger
may make hyenas of the best of us;

let us, therefore (though we do not forget
Love, the Creator,

her chariot and white doves),
entreat Hest,

Aset, Isis, the great enchantress,
in her attribute of Serqet,

the original great-mother,
who drove

harnessed scorpions
before her.

[35]

Let us substitute
enchantment for sentiment,

re-dedicate our gifts
to spiritual realism,

scrape a palette,
point pen or brush,

prepare papyrus or parchment,
offer incense to Thoth,

the original Ancient-of-days,
Hermes-thrice-great,

let us entreat
that he, by his tau-cross,

invoke the true-magic,
lead us back to the one-truth,

let him (Wisdom),
in the light of what went before,

illuminate what came after,
re-vivify the eternal verity,

be ye wise
as asps, scorpions, *as serpents.*

[36]

In no wise is the pillar-of-fire
that went before

different from the pillar-of-fire
that comes after;

chasm, schism in consciousness
must be bridged over;

we are each, householder,
each with a treasure;

now is the time to re-value
our secret hoard

in the light of both past and future,
for whether

coins, gems, gold
beakers, platters,

or merely
talismans, records or parchments,

explicitly, we are told,
it contains

for every scribe
which is instructed,

things new
and old.

[37]

Thou shalt have none other gods but me;
not on the sea

shall we entreat Triton or Dolphin,
not on the land

shall we lift rapt face and clasp hands
before laurel or oak-tree,

not in the sky
shall we invoke separately

Orion or Sirius
or the followers of the Bear,

not in the higher air
of Algorab, Regulus or Deneb

shall we cry
for help—or shall we?

[38]

This search for historical parallels,
research into psychic affinities,

has been done to death before,
will be done again;

no comment can alter spiritual realities
(you say) or again,

what new light can you possibly
throw upon them?

my mind (yours),
your way of thought (mine),

each has its peculiar intricate map,
threads weave over and under

the jungle-growth
of biological aptitudes,

inherited tendencies,
the intellectual effort

of the whole race,
its tide and ebb;

but my mind (yours)
has its peculiar ego-centric

personal approach
to the eternal realities,

and differs from every other
in minute particulars,

as the vein-paths on any leaf
differ from those of every other leaf

in the forest, as every snow-flake
has its particular star, coral or prism shape.

[39]

We have had too much consecration,
too little affirmation,

too much: but this, this, this
has been proved heretical,

too little: I know, I feel
the meaning that words hide;

they are anagrams, cryptograms,
little boxes, conditioned

to hatch butterflies . . .

[40]

For example:
Osiris equates O-sir-is or O-Sire-is;

Osiris,
the star Sirius,

relates resurrection myth
and resurrection reality

through the ages;
plasterer, crude mason,

not too well equipped, my thought
would cover deplorable gaps

in time, reveal the regrettable chasm,
bridge that before-and-after schism,

(before Abraham was I am)
uncover cankerous growths

in present-day philosophy,
in an endeavour to make ready,

as it were, the patient for the Healer;
correlate faith with faith,

recover the secret of Isis,
which is: there was One

in the beginning, Creator,
Fosterer, Begetter, the Same-forever

in the papyrus-swamp
in the Judean meadow.

[41]

Sirius:
what mystery is this?

you are seed,
corn near the sand,
enclosed in black-lead,
ploughed land.

Sirius:
what mystery is this?

you are drowned
in the river;
the spring freshets
push open the water-gates.

Sirius:
what mystery is this?

where heat breaks and cracks
the sand-waste,
you are a mist
of snow: white, little flowers.

[42]

O, Sire, is this the path?
over sedge, over dune-grass,

silently
sledge-runners pass.

O, Sire, is this the waste?
unbelievably,

sand glistens like ice,
cold, cold;

drawn to the temple-gate, O, Sire,
is this union at last?

[43]

Still the walls do not fall,
I do not know why;

there is zrr-hiss,
lightning in a not-known,

unregistered dimension;
we are powerless,

dust and powder fill our lungs
our bodies blunder

through doors twisted on hinges,
and the lintels slant

cross-wise;
we walk continually

on thin air
that thickens to a blind fog,

then step swiftly aside,
for even the air

is independable,
thick where it should be fine

and tenuous
where wings separate and open,

and the ether
is heavier than the floor,

and the floor sags
like a ship floundering;

we know no rule
of procedure,

we are voyagers, discoverers
of the not-known,

the unrecorded;
we have no map;

possibly we will reach haven,
heaven.

TRIBUTE TO THE ANGELS

To Osbert Sitwell

. . . possibly we will reach haven,
heaven.

[1]

Hermes Trismegistus
is patron of alchemists;

his province is thought,
inventive, artful and curious;

his metal is quicksilver,
his clients, orators, thieves and poets;

steal then, O orator,
plunder, O poet,

take what the old-church
found in Mithra's tomb,

candle and script and bell,
take what the new-church spat upon

and broke and shattered;
collect the fragments of the splintered glass

and of your fire and breath,
melt down and integrate,

re-invoke, re-create
opal, onyx, obsidian,

now scattered in the shards
men tread upon.

[2]

Your walls do not fall, he said,
because your walls are made of jasper;

but not four-square, I thought,
another shape (octahedron?)

slipped into the place
reserved by rule and rite

for the *twelve foundations*,
for the *transparent glass*,

for *no need of the sun*
nor *moon to shine*;

for the vision as we see
or have seen or imagined it

or in the past invoked
or conjured up or had conjured

by another, was usurped;
I saw the shape

which might have been of jasper,
but it was not four-square.

[3]

I John saw. I testify;
if any man shall add

God shall add unto him the plagues,
but he that sat upon the throne said,

I make all things new.
I John saw. I testify,

but *I make all things new,*
said He of the seven stars,

he of the seventy-times-seven
passionate, bitter wrongs,

He of the seventy-times-seven
bitter, unending wars.

[4]

Not in our time, O Lord,
the plowshare for the sword,

not in our time, the knife,
sated with life-blood and life,

to trim the barren vine;
no grape-leaf for the thorn,

no vine-flower for the crown;
not in our time, O King,

the voice to quell the re-gathering,
thundering storm.

[5]

Nay—*peace be still—*
lovest thou not Azrael,

the last and greatest, Death?
lovest not the sun,

the first who giveth life,
Raphael? *lovest thou me?*

lover of sand and shell,
know who withdraws the veil,

holds back the tide and shapes
shells to the wave-shapes? Gabriel:

Raphael, Gabriel, Azrael,
three of seven—what is War

to Birth, to Change, to Death?
yet he, red-fire is one of seven fires,

judgement and will of God,
God's very breath—Uriel.

[6]

Never in Rome,
so many martyrs fell;

not in Jerusalem,
never in Thebes,

so many stood and watched
chariot-wheels turning,

saw with their very eyes,
the battle of the Titans,

saw Zeus' thunderbolts in action
and how from giant hands,

the lightning shattered earth
and splintered sky, nor fled

to hide in caves,
but with unbroken will,

with unbowed head, watched
and though unaware, worshipped

and knew not that they worshipped
and that they were

that which they worshipped,
had they known the fire

of strength, endurance, anger
in their hearts,

was part of that same fire
that in a candle on a candle-stick

or in a star,
is known as one of seven,

is named among the seven Angels,
Uriel.

[7]

To Uriel, no shrine, no temple
where the red-death fell,

no image by the city-gate,
no torch to shine across the water,

no new fane in the market-place:
the lane is empty but the levelled wall

is purple as with purple spread
upon an altar,

this is the flowering of the rood,
this is the flowering of the reed,

where, Uriel, we pause to give
thanks that we rise again from death and live.

[8]

Now polish the crucible
and in the bowl distill

a word most bitter, *marah*,
a word bitterer still, *mar*,

sea, brine, breaker, seducer,
giver of life, giver of tears;

Now polish the crucible
and set the jet of flame

under, till *marah-mar*
are melted, fuse and join

and change and alter,
mer, mere, mère, mater, Maia, Mary,

Star of the Sea,
Mother.

[9]

Bitter, bitter jewel
in the heart of the bowl,

what is your colour?
what do you offer

to us who rebel?
what were we had you loved other?

what is this mother-father
to tear at our entrails?

what is this unsatisfied duality
which you can not satisfy?

[10]

In the field-furrow
the rain-water

showed splintered edge
as of a broken mirror,

and in the glass
as in a polished spear,

glowed the star Hesperus,
white, far and luminous,

incandescent and near,
Venus, Aphrodite, Astarte,

star of the east,
star of the west,

Phosphorus at sun-rise,
Hesperus at sun-set.

[11]

O swiftly, re-light the flame
before the substance cool,

for suddenly we saw your name
desecrated; knaves and fools

have done you impious wrong,
Venus, for venery stands for impurity

and Venus as desire
is venereous, lascivious,

while the very root of the word shrieks
like a mandrake when foul witches pull

its stem at midnight,
and rare mandragora itself

is full, they say, of poison,
food for the witches' den.

[12]

Swiftly re-light the flame,
Aphrodite, holy name,

Astarte, hull and spar
of wrecked ships lost your star,

forgot the light at dusk,
forgot the prayer at dawn;

return, O holiest one,
Venus whose name is kin

to venerate,
venerator.

[13]

"What is the jewel colour?"
green-white, opalescent,

with under-layer of changing blue,
with rose-vein; a white agate

with a pulse uncooled that beats yet,
faint blue-violet;

it lives, it breathes,
it gives off—fragrance?

I do not know what it gives,
a vibration that we can not name

for there is no name for it;
my patron said, "name it";

I said, I can not name it,
there is no name;

he said,
"invent it".

[14]

I can not invent it,
I said it was agate,

I said, it lived, it gave—
fragrance—was near enough

to explain that quality
for which there is no name;

I do not want to name it,
I want to watch its faint

heart-beat, pulse-beat
as it quivers, I do not want

to talk about it,
I want to minimize thought,

concentrate on it
till I shrink,

dematerialize
and am drawn into it.

[15]

Annael—this was another voice,
hardly a voice, a breath, a whisper,

and I remembered bell-notes,
Azrael, Gabriel, Raphael,

as when in Venice, one of the campanili
speaks and another answers,

until it seems the whole city (Venice-Venus)
will be covered with gold pollen shaken

from the bell-towers, lilies plundered
with the weight of massive bees . . .

[16]

Annael—and I remembered the sea-shell
and I remembered the empty lane

and I thought again of people,
daring the blinding rage

of the lightning, and I thought,
there is no shrine, no temple

in the city for that other, *Uriel*,
and I knew his companion,

companion of the fire-to-endure
was another fire, another candle,

was another of seven,
named among the seven Angels,

Annael,
peace of God.

[17]

So we hail them together,
one to contrast the other,

two of the seven Spirits,
set before God

as lamps on the high-altar,
for one must inexorably

take fire from the other
as spring from winter,

and surely never, never
was a spring more bountiful

than this; never, never
was a season more beautiful,

richer in leaf and colour;
tell me, in what other place

will you find the may flowering
mulberry and rose-purple?

tell me, in what other city
will you find the may-tree

so delicate, green-white, opalescent
like our jewel in the crucible?

[18]

For Uriel, no temple
but everywhere,

the outer precincts and the squares
are fragrant;

the festival opens as before
with the dove's murmuring;

for Uriel, no temple
but Love's sacred groves,

withered in Thebes and Tyre,
flower elsewhere.

[19]

We see her visible and actual,
beauty incarnate,

as no high-priest of Astoroth
could compel her

with incense
and potent spell;

we asked for no sign
but she gave a sign unto us;

sealed with the seal of death,
we thought not to entreat her

but prepared us for burial;
then she set a charred tree before us,

burnt and stricken to the heart;
was it may-tree or apple?

[20]

Invisible, indivisible Spirit,
how is it you come so near,

how is it that we dare
approach the high-altar?

we crossed the charred portico,
passed through a frame—doorless—

entered a shrine; like a ghost,
we entered a house through a wall;

then still not knowing
whether (like the wall)

we were there or not-there,
we saw the tree flowering;

it was an ordinary tree
in an old garden-square.

[21]

This is no rune nor riddle,
it is happening everywhere;

what I mean is—it is so simple
yet no trick of the pen or brush

could capture that impression;
music could do nothing with it,

nothing whatever; what I mean is—
but you have seen for yourself

that burnt-out wood crumbling . . .
you have seen for yourself.

[22]

A new sensation
is not granted to everyone,

not to everyone everywhere,
but to us here, a new sensation

strikes paralysing,
strikes dumb,

strikes the senses numb,
sets the nerves quivering;

I am sure you see
what I mean;

it was an old tree
such as we see everywhere,

anywhere here—and some barrel staves
and some bricks

and an edge of the wall
uncovered and the naked ugliness

and then . . . music? O, what I meant
by music when I said music, was—

music sets up ladders,
it makes us invisible,

it sets us apart,
it lets us escape;

but from the visible
there is no escape;

there is no escape from the spear
that pierces the heart.

[23]

We are part of it;
we admit the transubstantiation,

not God merely in bread
but God in the other-half of the tree

that looked dead—
did I bow my head?

did I weep? my eyes saw,
it was not a dream

yet it was vision,
it was a sign,

it was *the Angel which redeemed me,*
it was the Holy Ghost—

a half-burnt-out apple-tree
blossoming;

this is the flowering of the rood,
this is the flowering of the wood

where Annael, we pause to give
thanks that we rise again from death and live.

[24]

Every hour, every moment
has its specific attendant Spirit;

the clock-hand, minute by minute,
ticks round its prescribed orbit;

but this curious mechanical perfection
should not separate but relate rather,

our life, this temporary eclipse
to that other . . .

[25]

. . . of the *no need*
of the moon to shine in it,

for it was ticking minute by minute
(the clock at my bed-head,

with its dim, luminous disc)
when the Lady knocked;

I was talking casually
with friends in the other room,

when we saw the outer hall
grow lighter—then we saw where the door was,

there was no door
(this was a dream of course),

and she was standing there,
actually, at the turn of the stair.

[26]

One of us said, how odd,
she is actually standing there,

I wonder what brought her?
another of us said,

have we some power between us,
we three together,

that acts as a sort of magnet,
that attracts the super-natural?

(yet it was all natural enough,
we agreed);

I do not know what I said
or if I said anything,

for before I had time to speak,
I realized I had been dreaming,

that I lay awake now on my bed,
that the luminous light

was the phosphorescent face
of my little clock

and the faint knocking
was the clock ticking.

[27]

And yet in some very subtle way,
she was there more than ever,

as if she had miraculously
related herself to time here,

which is no easy trick, difficult
even for the experienced stranger,

of whom we must *be not forgetful*
for *some have entertained angels unawares.*

[28]

I had been thinking of Gabriel,
of the moon-cycle, of the moon-shell,

of the moon-crescent
and the moon at full:

I had been thinking of Gabriel,
the moon-regent, the Angel,

and I had intended to recall him
in the sequence of candle and fire

and the law of the seven;
I had not forgotten

his special attribute
of annunciator; I had thought

to address him as I had the others,
Uriel, Annael;

how could I imagine
the Lady herself would come instead?

[29]

We have seen her
the world over,

Our Lady of the Goldfinch,
Our Lady of the Candelabra,

Our Lady of the Pomegranate,
Our Lady of the Chair;

we have seen her, an empress,
magnificent in pomp and grace,

and we have seen her
with a single flower

or a cluster of garden-pinks
in a glass beside her;

we have seen her snood
drawn over her hair,

or her face set in profile
with the blue hood and stars;

we have seen her head bowed down
with the weight of a domed crown,

or we have seen her, a wisp of a girl
trapped in a golden halo;

we have seen her with arrow, with doves
and a heart like a valentine;

we have seen her in fine silks imported
from all over the Levant,

and hung with pearls brought
from the city of Constantine;

we have seen her sleeve
of every imaginable shade

of damask and figured brocade;
it is true,

the painters did very well by her;
it is true, they missed never a line

of the suave turn of the head
or subtle shade of lowered eye-lid

or eye-lids half-raised; you find
her everywhere (or did find),

in cathedral, museum, cloister,
at the turn of the palace stair.

[30]

We see her hand in her lap,
smoothing the apple-green

or the apple-russet silk;
we see her hand at her throat,

fingering a talisman
brought by a crusader from Jerusalem;

we see her hand unknot a Syrian veil
or lay down a Venetian shawl

on a polished table that reflects
half a miniature broken column;

we see her stare past a mirror
through an open window,

where boat follows slow boat on the lagoon;
there are white flowers on the water.

[31]

But none of these, none of these
suggest her as I saw her,

though we approach possibly
something of her cool beneficence

in the gracious friendliness
of the marble sea-maids in Venice,

who climb the altar-stair
at *Santa Maria dei Miracoli*,

or we acclaim her in the name
of another in Vienna,

Maria von dem Schnee,
Our Lady of the Snow.

[32]

For I can say truthfully,
her veils were *white as snow,*

so as no fuller on earth
can white them; I can say

she looked beautiful, she looked lovely,
she was *clothed with a garment*

down to the foot, but it was not
girt about with a golden girdle,

there was no gold, no colour
there was no gleam in the stuff

nor shadow of hem and seam,
as it fell to the floor; she bore

none of her usual attributes;
the Child was not with her.

[33]

Hermes took his attribute
of Leader-of-the-dead from Thoth

and the T-cross becomes caduceus;
the old-church makes its invocation

to Saint Michael and Our Lady
at the death-bed; Hermes Trismegistus

spears, with Saint Michael,
the darkness of ignorance,

casts the Old Dragon
into the abyss.

[34]

So Saint Michael,
regent of the planet Mercury,

is not absent
when we summon the other Angels,

another candle appears
on the high-altar,

it burns with a potent flame
but quivers

and quickens and darkens
and quickens again;

remember, it was Thoth
with a feather

who weighed the souls
of the dead.

[35]

So she must have been pleased with us,
who did not forgo our heritage

at the grave-edge;
she must have been pleased

with the straggling company of the brush and quill
who did not deny their birthright;

she must have been pleased with us,
for she looked so kindly at us

under her drift of veils,
and she carried a book.

[36]

Ah (you say), this is Holy Wisdom,
Santa Sophia, the SS of the *Sanctus Spiritus*,

so by facile reasoning, logically
the incarnate symbol of the Holy Ghost;

your Holy Ghost was an apple-tree
smouldering—or rather now bourgeoning

with flowers; the fruit of the Tree?
this is the new Eve who comes

clearly to return, to retrieve
what she lost the race,

given over to sin, to death;
she brings the Book of Life, obviously.

[37]

This is a symbol of beauty (you continue),
she is Our Lady universally,

I see her as you project her,
not out of place

flanked by Corinthian capitals,
or in a Coptic nave,

or frozen above the centre door
of a Gothic cathedral;

you have done very well by her
(to repeat your own phrase),

you have carved her tall and unmistakable,
a hieratic figure, the veiled Goddess,

whether of the seven delights,
whether of the seven spear-points.

[38]

O yes—you understand, I say,
this is all most satisfactory,

but she wasn't hieratic, she wasn't frozen,
she wasn't very tall;

she is the Vestal
from the days of Numa,

she carries over the cult
of the *Bona Dea*,

she carries a book but it is not
the tome of the ancient wisdom,

the pages, I imagine, are the blank pages
of the unwritten volume of the new;

all you say, is implicit,
all that and much more;

but she is not shut up in a cave
like a Sibyl; she is not

imprisoned in leaden bars
in a coloured window;

she is Psyche, the butterfly,
out of the cocoon.

[39]

But nearer than Guardian Angel
or good Daemon,

she is the counter-coin-side
of primitive terror;

she is not-fear, she is not-war,
but she is no symbolic figure

of peace, charity, chastity, goodness,
faith, hope, reward;

she is not Justice with eyes
blindfolded like Love's;

I grant you the dove's symbolic purity,
I grant you her face was innocent

and immaculate and her veils
like the Lamb's Bride,

but the Lamb was not with her,
either as Bridegroom or Child;

her attention is undivided,
we are her bridegroom and lamb;

her book is our book; written
or unwritten, its pages will reveal

a tale of a Fisherman,
a tale of a jar or jars,

the same—different—the same attributes,
different yet the same as before.

[40]

This is no rune nor symbol,
what I mean is—it is so simple

yet no trick of the pen or brush
could capture that impression;

what I wanted to indicate was
a new phase, a new distinction of colour;

I wanted to say, I did say
there was no sheen, no reflection,

no shadow; when I said white,
I did not mean sculptor's or painter's white,

nor porcelain; dim-white could
not suggest it, for when

is fresh-fallen snow (or snow
in the act of falling) dim?

yet even now, we stumble, we are lost—
what can we say?

she was not impalpable like a ghost,
she was not awe-inspiring like a Spirit,

she was not even over-whelming
like an Angel.

[41]

She carried a book, either to imply
she was one of us, with us,

or to suggest she was satisfied
with our purpose, a tribute to the Angels;

yet though the campanili spoke,
Gabriel, Azrael,

though the campanili answered,
Raphael, Uriel,

thought a distant note over-water
chimed *Annael*, and *Michael*

was implicit from the beginning,
another, deep, un-named, resurging bell

answered, sounding through them all:
remember, where there was

no need of the moon to shine . . .
I saw no temple.

Some call that deep-deep bell
Zadkiel, the righteousness of God,

he is regent of Jupiter
or Zeus-pater or Theus-pater,

Theus, God; God-the-father, father-god
or the Angel god-father,

himself, heaven yet at home in a star
whose colour is amethyst,

whose candle burns deep-violet
with the others.

[43]

And the point in the spectrum
where all lights become one,

is white and white is not no-colour,
as we were told as children

but all-colour;
where the flames mingle

and the wings meet, when we gain
the arc of perfection,

we are satisfied, we are happy,
we begin again;

I John saw. I testify
to rainbow feathers, to the span of heaven

and walls of colour,
the colonnades of jasper;

but when the jewel
melts in the crucible,

we find not ashes, not ash-of-rose,
not a tall vase and a staff of lilies,

not *vas spirituale,*
not *rosa mystica* even,

but a cluster of garden-pinks
or a face like a Christmas-rose.

This is the flowering of the rod,
this is the flowering of the burnt-out wood,

where, Zadkiel, we pause to give
thanks that we rise again from death and live.

London
May 17-31, 1944.

THE FLOWERING OF THE ROD

To Norman Holmes Pearson

. . . pause to give
thanks that we rise again from death and live.

[1]

O the beautiful garment,
the beautiful raiment—

do not think of His face
or even His hands,

do not think how we will stand
before Him;

remember the snow
on Hermon;

do not look below
where the blue gentian

reflects geometric pattern
in the ice-floe;

do not be beguiled
by the geometry of perfection

for even now,
the terrible banner

darkens the bridge-head;
we have shown

that we could stand;
we have withstood

the anger, frustration,
bitter fire of destruction;

leave the smouldering cities below
(we have done all we could),

we have given until we have no more to give;
alas, it was pity, rather than love, we gave;

now having given all, let us leave all;
above all, let us leave pity

and mount higher
to love—resurrection.

[2]

I go where I love and where I am loved,
into the snow;

I go to the things I love
with no thought of duty or pity;

I go where I belong, inexorably,
as the rain that has lain long

in the furrow; I have given
or would have given

life to the grain;
but if it will not grow or ripen

with the rain of beauty,
the rain will return to the cloud;

the harvester sharpens his steel on the stone;
but this is not our field,

we have not sown this;
pitiless, pitiless, let us leave

The-place-of-a-skull
to those who have fashioned it.

[3]

In resurrection, there is confusion
if we start to argue; if we stand and stare,

we do not know where to go;
in resurrection, there is simple affirmation,

but do not delay to round up the others,
up and down the street; your going

in a moment like this, is the best proof
that you know the way;

does the first wild-goose stop to explain
to the others? no—he is off;

they follow or not
that is their affair;

does the first wild-goose care
whether the others follow or not?

I don't think so—he is so happy to be off—
he knows where he is going;

so we must be drawn or we must fly,
like the snow-geese of the Arctic circle,

to the Carolinas or to Florida,
or like those migratory flocks

who still (they say) hover
over the lost island, Atlantis;

seeking what we once knew,
we know ultimately we will find

happiness; *to-day shalt thou be
with me in Paradise.*

[4]

Blue-geese, white-geese, you may say,
yes, I know this duality, this double nostalgia;

I know the insatiable longing
in winter, for palm-shadow

and sand and burnt sea-drift;
but in the summer, as I watch

the wave till its edge of foam
touches the hot sand and instantly

vanishes like snow on the equator,
I would cry out, stay, stay;

then I remember delicate enduring frost
and its mid-winter dawn-pattern;

in the hot noon-sun, I think of the grey
opalescent winter-dawn; as the wave

burns on the shingle, I think,
you are less beautiful than frost;

but it is also true that I pray,
O, give me burning blue

and brittle burnt sea-weed
above the tide-line,

as I stand, still unsatisfied,
under the long shadow-on-snow of the pine.

[5]

Satisfied, unsatisfied,
satiated or numb with hunger,

this is the eternal urge,
this is the despair, the desire to equilibrate

the eternal variant;
you understand that insistent calling,

that demand of a given moment,
the will to enjoy, the will to live,

not merely the will to endure,
the will to flight, the will to achievement,

the will to rest after long flight;
but who knows the desperate urge

of those others—actual or perhaps now
mythical birds—who seek but find no rest

till they drop from the highest point of the spiral
or fall from the innermost centre of the ever-
 narrowing circle?

for they remember, they remember, as they sway
 and hover,
what once was—they remember, they remember—

they will not swerve—they have known bliss,
the fruit that satisfies—they have come back—

what if the islands are lost? what if the waters
cover the Hesperides? they would rather
    remember—

remember the golden apple-trees;
O, do not pity them, as you watch them drop
    one by one,

for they fall exhausted, numb, blind
but in certain ecstasy,

for theirs is the hunger
for Paradise.

[6]

So I would rather drown, remembering—
than bask on tropic atolls

in the coral-seas; I would rather drown
remembering—than rest on pine or fir-branch

where great stars pour down
their generating strength, Arcturus

or the sapphires of the Northern Crown;
I would rather beat in the wind, crying to these
    others:

yours is the more foolish circling,
yours is the senseless wheeling

round and round—yours has no reason—
I am seeking heaven;

yours has no vision,
I see what is beneath me, what is above me,

what men say is-not—I remember,
I remember, I remember—you have forgot:

you think, even before it is half-over,
that your cycle is at an end,

but you repeat your foolish circling—again,
    again, again;
again, the steel sharpened on the stone;

again, the pyramid of skulls;
I gave pity to the dead,

O blasphemy, pity is a stone for bread,
only love is holy and love's ecstasy

that turns and turns and turns about one centre,
reckless, regardless, blind to reality,

that knows the Islands of the Blest are there,
for *many waters can not quench love's fire.*

[7]

Yet resurrection is a sense of direction,
resurrection is a bee-line,

straight to the horde and plunder,
the treasure, the store-room,

the honeycomb;
resurrection is remuneration,

food, shelter, fragrance
of myrrh and balm.

[8]

I am so happy,
I am the first or the last

of a flock or a swarm;
I am *full of new wine;*

I am branded with a word,
I am burnt with wood,

drawn from glowing ember,
not cut, not marked with steel;

I am the first or the last to renounce
iron, steel, metal;

I have gone forward,
I have gone backward,

I have gone onward from bronze and iron,
into the Golden Age.

[9]

No poetic fantasy
but a biological reality,

a fact: I am an entity
like bird, insect, plant

or sea-plant cell;
I live; I am alive;

take care, do not know me,
deny me, do not recognise me,

shun me; for this reality
is infectious—ecstasy.

[10]

It is no madness to say
you will fall, you great cities,

(now the cities lie broken);
it is not tragedy, prophecy

from a frozen Priestess,
a lonely Pythoness

who chants, who sings
in broken hexameters,

doom, doom to city-gates,
to rulers, to kingdoms;

it is simple reckoning, algebraic,
it is geometry on the wing,

not patterned, a gentian
in an ice-mirror,

yet it is, if you like, a lily
folded like a pyramid,

a flower-cone,
not a heap of skulls;

it is a lily, if you will,
each petal, a kingdom, an aeon,

and it is the seed of a lily
that having flowered,

will flower again;
it is that smallest grain,

the least of all seeds
that grows branches

where the birds rest;
it is that flowering balm,

it is heal-all,
everlasting;

it is the greatest among herbs
and becometh a tree.

[11]

He was the first that flew
(the heavenly pointer)

but not content to leave
the scattered flock,

He journeys back and forth
between the poles of heaven and earth forever;

He was the first to wing
from that sad Tree,

but having flown, the Tree of Life
bears rose from thorn

and fragrant vine,
from barren wood;

He was the first to say,
not to the chosen few,

his faithful friends,
the wise and good,

but to an outcast and a vagabond,
to-day shalt thou be with me in Paradise.

So the first—it is written,
will be the twisted or the tortured individuals,

out of line, out of step with world so-called
progress;
the first to receive the promise was a thief;

the first actually to witness His life-after-death,
was an unbalanced, neurotic woman,

who was naturally reviled for having left home
and not caring for house-work . . . or was that
Mary of Bethany?

in any case—as to this other Mary
and what she did, everyone knows,

but it is not on record
exactly where and how she found the alabaster jar;

some say she took the house-money
or the poor-box money,

some say she had nothing with her,
neither purse nor script,

no gold-piece or silver
stamped with image of Caesar.

[13]

In any case, she struck an uncanny bargain
(or so some say) with an Arab,

a stranger in the market-place;
actually, he had a little booth of a house

set to the left, back of the market
as you pass through the lower-gate;

what he had, was not for sale; he was on his way
to a coronation and a funeral—a double affair—

what he had, his priceless, unobtainable-elsewhere
        myrrh
was for the double ceremony, a funeral and a
        throning;

his was not ordinary myrrh and incense
and anyway, it is not for sale, he said;

he drew aside his robe in a noble manner
but the un-maidenly woman did not take the hint;

she had seen nobility herself at first hand;
nothing impressed her, it was easy to see;

she simply didn't care whether he acclaimed
or snubbed her—or worse; what are insults?

she knew how to detach herself,
another unforgivable sin,

and when stones were hurled,
she simply wasn't there;

she wasn't there and then she appeared,
not a beautiful woman really—would you say?

certainly not pretty;
what struck the Arab was that she was unpredictable;

this had never happened before—a woman—
well yes—if anyone did, he knew the world—a lady

had not taken a hint, had not sidled gracefully
at a gesture of implied dismissal

and with no apparent offence really,
out of the door.

[14]

It was easy to see that he was not an ordinary
 merchant;
she saw that certainly—he was an ambassador;

there was hardly anyone you could trust
with this precious merchandise,

though the jars were sealed,
the fragrance got out somehow,

and the rumour was bruited about,
even if you yourself managed to keep out

of the ordinary haunts of the merchants;
some said, this distillation, this attar

lasted literally forever, had so lasted—
though no one could of course, actually know

what was or was-not in those alabaster boxes
of the Princesses of the Hyksos Kings,

there were unguent jars, certainly;
but who would open them?

they had charms wrought upon them,
there were sigils and painted figures on all the jars;

no one dismantled the tombs,
that would be wickedness—but this he knew,

his own people for centuries and centuries,
had whispered the secret of the sacred processes of
distillation;

it was never written, not even in symbols, for this
they knew—
no secret was safe with a woman.

[15]

She said, I have heard of you;
he bowed ironically and ironically murmured,

I have not had the pleasure,
his eyes now fixed on the half-open door;

she understood; this was his second rebuff
but deliberately, she shut the door;

she stood with her back against it;
planted there, she flung out her arms,

a further barrier,
and her scarf slipped to the floor;

her face was very pale,
her eyes darker and larger

than many whose luminous depth
had inspired some not-inconsiderable poets;

but eyes? he had known many women—
it was her hair—un-maidenly—

It was hardly decent of her to stand there,
unveiled, in the house of a stranger.

[16]

I am Mary, she said, of a tower-town,
or once it must have been towered

for Magdala is a tower;
Magdala stands on the shore;

I am Mary, she said, of Magdala,
I am Mary, a great tower;

through my will and my power,
Mary shall be myrrh;

I am Mary—O, there are Marys a-plenty,
(though I am Mara, bitter) I shall be Mary-myrrh;

I am that myrrh-tree of the gentiles,
the heathen; there are idolaters,

even in Phrygia and Cappadocia,
who kneel before mutilated images

and burn incense to the Mother of Mutilations,
to Attis-Adonis-Tammuz and his mother who was
myrrh;

she was a stricken woman,
having borne a son in unhallowed fashion;

she wept bitterly till some heathen god
changed her to a myrrh-tree;

I am Mary, I will weep bitterly,
bitterly . . . bitterly.

[17]

But her voice was steady and her eyes were dry,
the room was small, hardly a room,

it was an alcove or a wide cupboard
with a closed door, a shaded window;

there was hardly any light from the window
but there seemed to be light somewhere,

as of moon-light on a lost river
or a sunken stream, seen in a dream

by a parched, dying man, lost in the desert . . .
or a mirage . . . it was her hair.

[18]

He who was unquestionably
master of caravans,

stooped to the floor;
he handed her her scarf;

it was unseemly that a woman
appear disordered, dishevelled;

it was unseemly that a woman
appear at all.

[19]

I am Mary, the incense-flower of the incense-tree,
myself worshipping, weeping, shall be changed to myrrh;

I am Mary, though melted away,
I shall be a tower . . . she said, Sir,

I have need, not of bread nor of wine,
nor of anything you can offer me,

and demurely, she knotted her scarf
and turned to unfasten the door.

[20]

Some say she slipped out and got away,
some say he followed her and found her,

some say he never found her
but sent a messenger after her

with the alabaster jar;
some say he himself was a Magician,

a Chaldean, not an Arab at all,
and had seen the beginning and the end,

that he was Balthasar, Melchior,
or that other of Bethlehem;

some say he was masquerading,
was an Angel in disguise

and had really arranged this meeting
to conform to the predicted pattern

which he or Balthasar or another
had computed exactly from the stars;

some say it never happened,
some say it happens over and over;

some say he was an old lover
of Mary Magdalene and the gift of the myrrh

was in recognition of an old burnt-out
yet somehow suddenly renewed infatuation;

some say he was Abraham,
some say he was God.

[21]

Anyhow, it is exactly written,
the house was filled with the odour of the ointment;

that was a little later and this was not such a small
house
and was maybe already fragrant with boughs and
wreaths,

for this was a banquet, a festival;
it was all very gay and there was laughter,

but Judas Iscariot turned down his mouth,
he muttered Extravagant under his breath,

for the nard though not potent,
had that subtle, indefinable essence

that lasts longer and costs more;
Judas whispered to his neighbour

and then they all began talking about the poor;
but Mary, seated on the floor,

like a child at a party, paid no attention;
she was busy; she was deftly un-weaving

the long, carefully-braided tresses
of her extraordinary hair.

[22]

But Simon the host thought,
we must draw the line somewhere;

he had seen something like this
in a heathen picture

or a carved stone-portal entrance
to a forbidden sea-temple;

they called the creature,
depicted like this,

seated on the sea-shore
or on a rock, a Siren,

a maid-of-the-sea, a mermaid;
some said, this mermaid sang

and that a Siren-song was fatal
and wrecks followed the wake of such hair;

she was not invited,
he bent to whisper

into the ear of his Guest,
I do not know her.

[23]

There was always a crowd hanging about outside
any door his Guest happened to enter;

he did not wish to make a scene,
he would call someone quietly to eject her;

Simon though over-wrought and excited,
had kept careful count of his guests;

things had gone excellently till now,
but this was embarrassing;

she was actually kissing His feet;
He does not understand;

they call him a Master,
but Simon questioned:

this man if he were a prophet, would have known
who and what manner of woman this is.

[24]

Simon did not know but Balthasar
or Melchior could have told him,

or better still, Gaspar or Kaspar,
who, they say, brought the myrrh;

Simon wished to avoid a scene
but Kaspar knew the scene was unavoidable

and already written in a star
or a configuration of stars

that rarely happens, perhaps once
in a little over two thousand years.

[25]

Simon could say, yes,
she looked like a heathen

picture or carved idol
from a forbidden sea-temple;

and Simon might have heard
that this woman from the city,

was devil-ridden or had been;
but Kaspar might call

the devils *daemons*,
and might even name the seven

under his breath, for technically
Kaspar was a heathen;

he might whisper tenderly, those names
without fear of eternal damnation,

Isis, Astarte, Cyprus
and the other four;

he might re-name them,
Ge-meter, De-meter, earth-mother

or Venus
in a star.

[26]

But it is not fair to compare
Kaspar with Simon;

this Simon is not Simon Peter, of course,
this is not Simon Zelotes, the Canaanite

nor Simon of Cyrene
nor the later Simon, the sorcerer,

this Simon is Simon, the leper;
but Simon being one of the band,

we presume was healed of his plague,
healed in body, while the other,

the un-maidenly mermaid, Mary of Magdala
was healed of soul; out of her, the Master

had cast seven devils;
but Simon, though healed of body,

was not conditioned to know
that these very devils or *daemons*,

as Kaspar would have called them,
were now unalterably part of the picture;

they had entered separately or together
the fair maid, perhaps not wantonly,

but crossing the threshold
of this not un-lovely temple,

they intended perhaps to pay homage,
even as Kaspar had done,

and Melchior
and Balthasar.

[27]

And Kaspar (for of course, the merchant was Kaspar)
did not at first know her;

she was frail and slender, wearing no bracelet
or other ornament, and with her scarf

wound round her head, draping her shoulders,
she was impersonal, not a servant

sent on an errand, but, as it were,
a confidential friend, sent by some great lady;

she was discretion itself
in her dark robe and head-dress;

Kaspar did not recognise her
until her scarf slipped to the floor,

and then, not only did he recognise Mary
as the stars had told (Venus in the ascendant

or Venus in conjunction with Jupiter,
or whatever he called these wandering fires),

but when he saw the light on her hair
like moonlight on a lost river,

Kaspar
remembered.

[28]

And Kaspar heard
an echo of an echo in a shell,
in her were forgiven
the sins of the seven
daemons cast out of her;

and Kaspar saw as in a mirror,
another head uncovered and two crowned,

one with a plain circlet, one with a circlet of gems
which even he could not name;

and Kaspar, master of caravans,
had known splendour such as few have known,

and seen jewels cut and un-cut that altered
like water at sun-rise and sun-set,

and blood-stones and sapphires;
we need no detailed statement of Kaspar's specific
knowledge

nor inventory of his own possessions,
all we need to know is that Kaspar

knew more about precious stones than any other,
more even than Balthasar;

but his heart was filled with a more exalted ecstasy
than any valuer over a new tint of rose or smoke-grey

in an Indian opal or pearl; this was Kaspar
who saw as in a mirror,

one head uncrowned and then one with a plain
head-band
and then one with a circlet of gems of an inimitable colour;

they were blue yet verging on purple,
yet very blue; if asked to describe them,

you would say they were blue stones
of a curious square cut and set so that the light

broke as if from within; the reflecting inner facets
seemed to cast incalculable angles of light,

this blue shot with violet;
how convey what he felt?

he saw as in a mirror, clearly, O very clearly,
a circlet of square-cut stones on the head of a lady,

and what he saw made his heart so glad
that it was as if he suffered,

his heart laboured so
with his ecstasy.

[29]

It was not solely because of beauty
though there was that too,

it was discovery, discovery that exalted him
for he knew the old tradition, the old, old legend,

his father had had from his grandfather
and his grandfather from his great-grandfather (and so
on),

was true; this was never spoken about, not even
whispered in secret;
the legend was contained in old signs and symbols,

and only the most painful application could decipher
them,
and only the very-few could even attempt to do this,

after boy-hood and youth dedicated
to the rigorous sessions of concentration

and study of the theme and law
of time-relation and retention of memory;

but in the end, Kaspar, too, received the title Magian
(it is translated in the Script, *Wise Man*).

[30]

As he stooped for the scarf, he saw this,
and as he straightened, in that half-second,

he saw the fleck of light
like a flaw in the third jewel

to his right, in the second circlet,
a grain, a flaw, or a speck of light,

and in that point or shadow,
was the whole secret of the mystery;

literally, as his hand just did-not touch her hand,
and as she drew the scarf toward her,

the speck, fleck, grain or seed
opened like a flower.

[31]

And the flower, thus contained
in the infinitely tiny grain or seed,

opened petal by petal, a circle,
and each petal was separate

yet still held, as it were,
by some force of attraction

to its dynamic centre;
and the circle went on widening

and would go on opening
he knew, to infinity;

but before he was lost,
out-of-time completely,

he saw the islands of the Blest,
he saw the Hesperides,

he saw the circles and circles of islands
about the lost centre-island, Atlantis;

he saw what the sacrosanct legend
said still existed,

he saw the lands of the blest,
the promised lands, lost;

he, in that half-second, saw
the whole scope and plan

of our and his civilization on this,
his and our earth, before Adam.

[32]

And he saw it all as if enlarged under a sun-glass;
he saw it all in minute detail,

the cliffs, the wharves, the citadel,
he saw the ships and the sea-roads crossing

and all the rivers and bridges and dwelling-houses
and the terraces and the built-up inner gardens;

he saw the many pillars and the Hearth-stone
and the very fire on the Great-hearth,

and through it, there was a sound as of many waters,
rivers flowing and fountains and sea-waves washing the
sea-rocks,

and though it was all on a very grand scale,
yet it was small and intimate,

Paradise
before Eve . . .

[33]

And he heard, as it were, the echo
of an echo in a shell,

words neither sung nor chanted
but stressed rhythmically;

the echoed syllables of this spell
conformed to the sound

of no word he had ever heard spoken,
and Kaspar was a great wanderer,

a renowned traveller;
but he understood the words

though the sound was other
than our ears are attuned to,

the tone was different
yet he understood it;

it translated itself
as it transmuted its message

through spiral upon spiral of the shell
of memory that yet connects us

with the drowned cities of pre-history;
Kaspar understood and his brain translated:

Lilith born before Eve
and one born before Lilith,
and Eve; we three are forgiven,
we are three of the seven
daemons cast out of her.

[34]

Then as he dropped his arm
in the second half-second,

his mind prompted him,
even as if his mind

must sharply differentiate,
clearly define the boundaries of beauty;

hedges and fences and fortresses
must defend the innermost secret,

even the hedges and fortresses of the mind;
so his mind thought,

though his spirit was elsewhere
and his body functioned, though himself,

he-himself was not there;
and his mind framed the thought,

the last inner defence
of a citadel, now lost,

it is unseemly that a woman
appear disordered, dishevelled,

it is unseemly that a woman
appear at all.

[35]

What he thought was the direct contradiction
of what he apprehended,

what he saw was a woman of discretion,
knotting a scarf,

and an unpredictable woman
sliding out of a door;

we do not know whether or not
he himself followed her

with the alabaster jar; all we know is,
the myrrh or the *spikenard, very costly,* was Kaspar's,

all we know is that it was all so very soon over,
the feasting, the laughter.

[36]

And the snow fell on Hermon,
the place of the Transfiguration,

and the snow fell on Hebron
where, last spring, the anemones grew,

whose scarlet and rose and red and blue,
He compared to a King's robes,

but *even Solomon,* He said,
was not arrayed like one of these;

and the snow fell on the almond-trees
and the mulberries were domed over

like a forester's hut or a shepherd's hut
on the slopes of Lebanon,

and the snow fell
silently . . . silently . . .

[37]

And as the snow fell on Hebron,
the desert blossomed as it had always done;

over-night, a million-million tiny plants
broke from the sand,

and a million-million little grass-stalks
each put out a tiny flower,

they were so small, you could hardly
visualize them separately,

so it came to be said,
snow falls on the desert;

it had happened before,
it would happen again.

[38]

And Kaspar grieved as always,
when a single twin of one of his many goats was
    lost—

such a tiny kid, not worth thinking about,
he was such a rich man, with numberless herds,
    cattle and sheep—

and he let the long-haired mountain-goats
return to the pasture earlier than usual,

for they chafed in their pens, sniffing the air
and the flowering-grass; and he himself watched all
    night

by his youngest white camel whose bearing was
    difficult,
and cherished the foal—it looked like a large white
    owl—

under his cloak and brought it to his tent
for shelter and warmth; that is how the legend got
    about

that Kaspar
was Abraham.

[39]

He was a very kind man
and he had numberless children,

but he was not Abraham come again;
he was the Magian Kaspar;

he said *I am Kaspar,*
for he had to hold on to something;

I am Kaspar, he said when a slender girl
holding a jar, asked deferentially

if she might lower it into his well;
I am Kaspar; if her head were veiled

and veiled it almost always would be,
he would remember, though never

for a moment did he quite forget
the turn of a wrist as it fastened a scarf,

the saffron-shape of the sandal,
the pleat of the robe, the fold of the garment

as Mary lifted the latch and the door half-parted,
and the door shut, and there was the flat door

at which he stared and stared,
as if the line of wood, the rough edge

or the polished surface or plain,
were each significant, as if each scratch and mark

were hieroglyph, a parchment of incredible worth
or a mariner's map.

[40]

And no one will ever know
whether the picture he saw clearly

as in a mirror was pre-determined
by his discipline and study

of old lore and by his innate capacity
for transcribing and translating

the difficult secret symbols,
no one will ever know how it happened

that in a second or a second and half a second,
he saw further, saw deeper, apprehended more

than anyone before or after him;
no one will ever know

whether it was a sort of spiritual optical-illusion,
or whether he looked down the deep deep-well

of the so-far unknown
depth of pre-history;

no one would ever know
if it could be proved mathematically

by demonstrated lines,
as an angle of light

reflected from a strand of a woman's hair,
reflected again or refracted

a certain other angle—
or perhaps it was a matter of vibration

that matched or caught an allied
or exactly opposite vibration

and created a sort of vacuum,
or rather a *point* in time—

he called it a fleck or flaw in a gem
of the crown that he saw

(or thought he saw) as in a mirror;
no one would know exactly

how it happened,
least of all Kaspar.

[41]

No one will know exactly how it came about,
but we are permitted to wonder

if it had possibly something to do
with the vow he had made—

well, it wasn't exactly a vow,
an idea, a wish, a whim, a premonition perhaps,

that premonition we all know,
this has happened before somewhere else,

or *this will happen again—where? when?*
for, as he placed his jar on the stable-floor,

he remembered old Azar . . . old Azar
had often told how, in the time of the sudden
winter-rain,

after the memorable autumn-drought,
the trees were mortally torn,

when the sudden frost came;
but Azar died while Kaspar was still a lad,

and whether Azar's tale referred
to the year of the yield of myrrh,

distilled in this very jar,
or another—Kaspar could not remember;

but Kaspar thought, there were always two jars,
the two were always together,

why didn't I bring both?
or should I have chosen the other?

for Kaspar remembered old, old Azar muttering,
other days and better ways, and it was always
    maintained

that one jar was better than the other,
but he grumbled and shook his head,

no one can tell which is which,
now your great-grandfather is dead.

[42]

It was only a thought,
someday I will bring the other,

as he placed his jar
on the floor of the ox-stall;

Balthasar had offered the spikenard,
Melchior, the rings of gold;

they were both somewhat older than Kaspar
so he stood a little apart,

as if his gift were an after-thought,
not to be compared with theirs;

when Balthasar had pushed open the stable-door
or gate, a shepherd was standing there,

well—a sort of shepherd, an older man with a staff,
perhaps a sort of night-watchman;

as Balthasar hesitated, he said, Sir,
I am afraid there is no room at the Inn,

as if to save them the trouble of coming further,
inquiring perhaps as to bedding-down

their valuable beasts; but Balthasar
acknowledged the gentle courtesy of the man

and passed on; and Balthasar entered the ox-stall,
and Balthasar touched his forehead and his breast,

as he did at the High Priest's side
before the Holy-Presence-Manifest;

and Balthasar spoke the Great Word,
and Balthasar bowed, as if the weight of this honour

bent him down, as if over-come
by this overwhelming Grace,

and Balthasar stood aside
and Melchior took his place.

And Melchior made gesture with his hands
as if in a dance or play,

to show without speaking, his unworthiness,
to indicate that this, his gift, was symbolic,

worthless in itself (those weighty rings of gold),
and Melchior bent and kissed the earth, speechless,

for this was the ritual
of the second order of the priests.

And Kaspar stood a little to one side
like an unimportant altar-servant,

and placed his gift
a little apart from the rest,

to show by inference
its unimportance in comparison;

and Kaspar stood
he inclined his head only slightly,

as if to show,
out of respect to the others,

these older, exceedingly honoured ones,
that his part in this ritual

was almost negligible,
for the others had bowed low.

[43]

But she spoke so he looked at her,
she was shy and simple and young;

she said, Sir, it is a most beautiful fragrance,
as of all flowering things together;

but Kaspar knew the seal of the jar was unbroken.
he did not know whether she knew

the fragrance came from the bundle of myrrh
she held in her arms.

London
December 18-31, 1944.

READERS' NOTES

The first number is the page, the second the line on the page. NHP is an abreviation for Norman Holmes Pearson's foreword to the first New Directions edition of *Trilogy,* and TF is an abbreviation for H.D.'s *Tribute to Freud* (New Directions, 1956).

THE WALLS DO NOT FALL

3.1 **Incident** During World War II, the newspapers called the air battles over the UK "incidents."

3.5 **Luxor bee, chick and hare** At Luxor, site of the ancient Egyptian city of Thebes, near the present village of Karnak, are the intact ruins of the Temple of Amon, the greatest monument of antiquity, built under the pharaoh Amenhotop III (1414–1397 B.C.). Amon is Ra, the Egyptian sun god. (See Ra, 25.1–4.) The **bee** in Egyptian mythology came from the tears of Ra. The **bee, chick,** and **hare** are all symbols of fertility and regeneration.

3.7 **in green, rose-red, lapis** In Egyptian writing, **green** is the color of fertility; Isis, a fertility goddess, is the Lady of the green Emerald (see Isis 5.18). The **rose** is also sacred to Isis. **Lapis** blue is associated with truth. Mummies were painted lapis blue to show that they were united with truth.

3.24 **old, Samuel** The prophet Samuel was the oldest judge and first prophet after Moses. First and Second Samuel are thought to be the oldest narrative books in the Bible and cover the careers of Samuel, Saul, and David.

4.3 **Pythian pronounces** The Pythian refers to the prophetess or oracle at the Temple of Apollo at Delphi (6th century B.C.) in Greece. Seated on a golden tripod, when questioned she uttered sounds in a frenzied trance interpreted by a priest who usually disclosed them in verse.

4.7 Pompeii A prosperous ancient Roman port city near Naples at the foot of Mount Vesuvius, which erupted in A.D. 79 and covered the city with volcanic lava, killing everyone, but also preserving all in the instant of eruption. The colorful wall paintings, domestic objects, and villas were also preserved, giving us the clearest picture of a day in Roman antiquity. The city was rediscovered in 1748. There was a cult of Isis in Pompeii. See 5.18.

4.13 Apocryphal fire The Apocrypha are the fourteen books of the Septuagint Greek Bible, excluded from the Protestant but included as secondarily canonical in the Catholic, Greek Orthodox, and Hebrew Bibles. Apocrypha signifies "of questionable authenticity," but here the usage actually suggests Apocalyptic fire, meaning the vision of Hell's fires in the Apocalypse or Revelation, the visionary last book of the New Testament.

5.8 manna-beans Manna is the food sent by God to the Children of Israel on their journey across the desert: "Then the Lord said unto Moses, Behold, I will rain bread from heaven for you" (Ex. 16.4). Some Jewish and Christian writers interpret manna as Logos. By the same token, manna is thought by some Christian theologians to prefigure the Eucharist.

5.13 gods always face two-ways The Roman god Janus, guardian of the gates and roads, is represented with two heads, facing two ways. He is the custodian of the universe. In times of peace the gates of his temple in the Roman Forum were closed, in times of war, they were open.

5.18 Isis, Aset or Astarte Isis, daughter of the sky goddess Nut and the earth god Geb, was sister and husband of Osiris, god of the underworld. Isis saved Osiris (see 25.1–4). She sewed him together after he had been slain and cut in many pieces. Isis was also a mother goddess, goddess of fertility, magic, and beauty, and widely worshiped for her ability to counter evil spells. The Greeks identified her with Athena and Demeter. Isis is often depicted suckling her baby son Horus; the iconography of sacred mother and child is said to be the model for Mary and Jesus. **Aset or Astarte.** Astarte was a Phoenician goddess of fertility, corresponding to earlier Babylonian Ishtar and later Greek

Aphrodite, goddess of love and beauty. In Assyrian-Babylonian art she caresses a child whom she holds in her left hand. Her other names are Ashtart and Ashtoreth.

7.1 Sceptre A sceptre or scepter is a staff of authority of god or human, and often a phallic symbol. For H.D. it is associated with the caduceus, a magic herald's rod that is winged and entwined by two snakes. Later in *Tribute to the Angels* and *The Flowering of the Rod,* the staff becomes Aaron's rod and the rood (or cross) of Christ. In Genesis the sceptre is already established as a symbol of divine and human authority: "The sceptre shall not depart from Judah" (Gen. 49.10). In Exodus, Moses assumes power through the rod: "and Moses took the rod of God in his hand" (Ex. 4.20). Aaron, brother of Moses and high priest, transforms the rod into a serpent to make it swallow the serpents of the Pharaoh and his magicians (Ex. 7.10–12), which served as a warning to the Pharaoh to release the people of Israel from bondage. Later in the desert, when the tribes are rebellious and looking to other gods, Aaron makes the rod blossom and bear almonds, thereby establishing the authority of Aaron as head of the tribe of Levi over the rebellious tribes in the desert (Num. 17.1–8). See 7.5, 70.9–10, and note for the title *The Flowering of the Rod* 111.

7.3 lily The lily is associated with purity, innocence, resurrection, chastity, the Virgin Mary, and Easter.

7.5 Caduceus The caduceus is a rod or wand carried by Hermes, the messenger god. It consists of a wing-topped staff, with two serpents winding around it. Hermes found two snakes fighting and put his rod between them. In another legend Apollo gives the caduceus to Hermes. For the Romans it became a symbol of neutrality or truce and was carried by heralds and ambassadors making them immune to attack. The intertwining snakes on a staff appear in Babylonia as a symbol of the sun gods, fertility, wisdom, and healing. In alchemy, it is the symbol of the union of opposing forces. Since the 16th century it has replaced Asklepios's one-snaked rod as a symbol of medicine, and since 1902 it has been the symbol of the medical branch of the US army. Asklepios was the son of Apollo and a healer who could raise the dead. His ability enraged Zeus and he killed him, but Apollo persuaded Zeus to make Asklepios the god of medicine. H.D. called Asklepios (and Freud) "the blameless physician" and wrote of the serpent: "The Serpent is certainly the sign or totem, through the ages, of healing and of that final healing when we slough off, for the last time, our encumbering flesh or skin. The serpent is the symbol of death, as we know, but also of resurrection" (TF 65). See 7.1, 70.9–10, and note for the title *The Flowering of the Rod* 111.

9.14–15 the whale // cannot digest me Refers to the story of Jonah and the whale in the book of Jonah. In the book of Jonah, God spares Nineveh after Jonah prophesies that it will be destroyed (see 24.18 for Nineveh).

9.24 pearl-of-great-price Jesus says: "Again the kingdom of heaven is like unto a merchant man, seeking goodly pearls: Who, when he found one pearl of great price, went and sold all that he had, and bought it. Again, the kingdom of heaven is like unto a net, that was cast into the sea, and gathered of every kind: Which, when it was full, they drew to shore, and sat down, and gathered the good into vessels, but cast the bad away. So shall it be at the end of the world the angels shall come forth, and sever the wicked from among the just." Matthew 13.45–49.

10.15–16 His, the Genius in the jar / which the fisherman finds The Genius probably puns on the Genie in the bottle or lamp. For **Fisherman** see 105.3.

10.17–18 He is Mage, / bringing myrrh. The Magi or three wise men brought gifts of gold, frankincense, and myrrh to the baby Jesus. Myrrh was used in emblaming and as an aphrodisiac, and is associated with immortality. H.D. sees myrrh as poetry because of its association with immortality, sacredness, and resurrection.

14.2 twin-horns, disk, erect serpent The Egyptian goddess Isis is depicted with a headdress of **twin horns** holding a sun **disk**. The sacred **erect serpent** Uraeus was a representative of the goddess and appeared on the headdress of Egyptian deities and rulers. In mythology, Isis, who was a mortal magician, attained godhood by fashioning a snake out of earth and the spittle of Ra. The snake bit Ra and Ra, who was in pain, asked Isis for help. She replied that she would help him only if he told her his true name. Though Ra tried to deceive Isis with false names, in the end he revealed it, and with this secret knowledge Isis became a goddess. See notes 7.1, 7.5, and about names, see 21.2

14.3 double-plume or lotus The **plume** adorns helmets and headdresses and is a symbol of social status. The **lotus** is the most common pattern of adornment in Egyptian art, and is the source of the lily ornamentation on capitals. The lotus is a water lily that draws into itself at night. In Egypt the lotus carries the sun within itself and arises from primeval waters, specifically the Nile, which is sacred and life-giving. The lotus is the flower on which Horus, Isis's son, is seated, and is associated with fertility, death, resurrection, and the sun.

15.7 **heron's crest** The **heron** or ibis, sacred to the Egyptians, is associated with secret knowledge and is said to have been the secretary to Thoth or Hermes Trismegistes (see 16.1). It is also associated with the phoenix or bennu bird, and like other serpent-eating animals is a Christ symbol.

15.8 **Asp** See 14.2.

16.1 **Thoth, Hermes** Thoth, the scribe of the gods of ancient Egypt, many of whose attributes Greek Hermes was later to take on, was creator and orderer of the universe, a god of magic, wisdom, learning, a patron of the arts, and, among other literary achievements he was the inventor of writing, letters, and the materials on which they are inscribed (such as papyrus and parchment). He is depicted as a man with an ibis head. As the god of magical knowledge, he later became identified with Hermes Trismegistus, the most significant Pagan Gnostic, whose hermetic writings probably represented a tradition rather than a single person.

16.15 **Hatshepsut** Hatshepsut was queen of ancient Egypt (1486–1468 B.C.). She ruled by relegating her husband to the shadow, and after his death she ruled as regent for their son. Her reign was peaceful and she developed economic resources.

16.16 **cartouche** The cartouche on Egyptian hieroglyphs is an oval or oblong figure that encloses characters of names or epithets of royal or divine personages.

17.5 **Mercury, Hermes, Thoth** The Roman, Greek, and Egyptian names, respectively, of the messenger God. See 16.1.

17.11 **O Sword** The guardian angel Michael carries a sword, but the triumph of the sword will soon be over, as we see in lines 15–16. "In the beginning was the word" are the first words of the Gospel of John. (See 17.15–16.) In these lines may be a resonance of the frequent New Testament statement that the New Testament will triumph over the Old. Given the evocation immediately before of Mercury, Hermes, Thoth, as gods of the word and pen, the clear meaning is that "the pen is mightier than the sword," a Latin expression that pops up in English, as in Edward Bulwer-Lytton's *Richelieu* (1839): "Beneath the rule of men entirely great / the pen is mightier than the sword" (Act 2, scene 2). See Michael 98.5, 98.7, 99.1.

17.15–16 in the beginning / was the Word The verse begins the Gospel of John. This Gnostic beginning of John is a paraphrase of the first line of Genesis. "In the beginning God created the world." The "word," or *logos,* first appears in Greek philosophy in the *Cosmic Fragments* of the pre-Socratic Heraclitus (c. 535–475). The notion that God creates the world with a word fits well with the Egyptian Thoth, who creates both the universe and the written word.

19.13 there was a whirr and roar in the high air Reference to the German airplanes and the bombing of London.

20.1–2 The Presence was spectrum-blue, / ultimate blue ray Blue is the color of truth (see 3.7) and of the divine. The Egyptian serpents of eternal wisdom are blue with yellow stripes. Blue is the color of Eden and eternal youth, the color of the stones of the Ten Commandments. The Virgin Mary's robes are depicted as blue.

21.2 Name In Eden Adam is the first name giver. "Adam gave names to all cattle, and to the fowl of the air, and to every beast of the field" (Gn. 4.20). The Egyptian belief that names correspond to aspects of the soul has been passed on to the Judeo-Christian tradition. Finding out the secret name of a god or mortal confers power onto the discoverer, as in the case of Isis and Ra. See 14.2.

22.9 the new Sun Ra is the Egyptian sun god. In Egypt, among the gods, the worship of Ra was the most widespread. Probably also a pun on the "Son" of God, Jesus Christ. See 25.1–4.

24.18 Nineveh and Babel Nineveh, near modern Mosul in Iraq, was the capital of the Assyrian Empire, powerful in the second millennium. It came to an end in 612 B.C. when it was defeated by a coalition of Babylonians, Medes, and Scythians. Babel was the site in the Bible where the descendants of Noah built a tower, trying to reach heaven. The destruction of the tower led to dispersal from Babel and the loss of a single world language. Babel is identified with Babylon. Nineveh and Babel, both destroyed, subsequently vanished.

25.1–4 Ra, Osiris, Amen appeared / in a spacious, bare meeting-house / he is the world-father, / father of past aeons In Egyptian religion Ra is the sun god, chief deity, creator of the cosmos and father of all things. Early Egyptian kings took his name and claimed descent from him. He is represented by the hawk and the lion. In Greek religion he is Apollo. Other gods are identified with him, mainly Amon as in Amon-Ra. **Amen** is a variation in name of Amon or Ammon. Amon's most important shrine was the Temple of Amon at Luxor in ancient Thebes. (See 3.5.) **Osiris** was god of the underworld and ruler of predynastic Egypt. He was brother and husband of Isis. After he was treacherously slain by his brother Set and cut up into fourteen pieces, according to one version, he was buried in diverse parts of Egypt, each of which became a sacred place. In another story, Isis gathered the fourteen pieces, sewed them together, and then he was resurrected into life. Osiris was seen as the culmination of the creative forces of nature and eternal life and therefore **the world father, father of past aeons.** He was identified with the sun, moon, the grain of the earth and the waters of the Nile. By introducing the "meeting house," H.D. also permits "the father of past aeons" to refer to earlier authority figures in her Quaker and Moravian experiences. The actual words "father of past aeons" seem to be a telescoped parody of the beginning and end of the Lord's Prayer in Matthew 6.9–13. Verse 6.9 asserts the heavenly station of the father, "our Father which art in heaven, Hallowed be thy name." The prayer ends (actually an "orphan" ending appended later to the passage) with the father's full control of the universe: "For thine is the kingdom, and the power, and the glory, forever. Amen." As a reader of Greek, H.D. knew that the Anglo-Saxon word "forever" is *aion* in N.T. Greek, and so, by inserting the correct Greek word, *aion*/aeons, into her epithet, she connects her Christian father figure with her mutable Egyptian god.

Norman Holmes Pearson identifies the "spacious bare meeting-house" as a Quaker meeting house. He writes, "Karnak and London were periods of H.D.'s history. So also were Bethlehem and Philadelphia, though they remain significant shadows in the *Trilogy*" (NHPxi). Though she was born, not insignificantly, in Bethlehem, Pennsylvania, an eighteenth-century early Moravian city, the Quaker influence was strong. Pearson observes, "Philadelphia was named by Penn certainly with *The Book of Revelation* in mind. The 'spacious, bare meeting-house' of her dream of the 'father of past aeons' in *The Walls,* she describes elsewhere as Quaker, 'in or by Philadelphia," where her family worshiped when she was in her 'teens, there being no Moravian congregation conveniently near" (NPH xi).

25.8 Memnon monolith In Greek mythology Memnon was the son of Tithonos (who like the sibyl of Cumae aged but could not die) and Eos, goddess of dawn. He was also king of Ethiopia. He fought in the Trojan war and was killed by Achilles, but Eos gained immortality for her son from Zeus. Memnon lived in Egypt and the Greeks gave his name to the great monolith statue of Amenhotep III, the builder of the Temple of Amon. Hence we have the Memnon monolith.

26.14 the new Sun The new Sun is a pun connecting the Sun God Ra with the New Son Jesus. H.D., among others, identifies Ra or Amon (Amen) with Jesus, and as in many prayers to Christ that end *forever and ever, Amen,* she puns on *amen* (from Hebrew *amen*), by capitalizing *amen,* thereby turning a Christian prayer into the regeneration of Egyptian Amon-ra. See 25.1–4.

27.1 Christos In Greek, **Christos** is the word for Christ, which means the anointed, and is a translation from Hebrew *mashiah,* meaning the Messiah.

28.1–2 the authentic Jew / stepped out from Velasquez "The authentic Jew" would be Jesus Christ as Yeshua the Messiah (his name from Aramaic), the crucified rabbi. Diego Velazquez (the Spanish painter, 1599–1660) painted a realistic "Christ on the Cross," for which the model might have been a *converso,* a Jew who became a "new Christian" after 1492.

29.17 Mage The Mage or Magi were Zoroastrian wise-men priests/astrologers from Persia. The word magic comes from Magus, the priest who was deft in magic. In Matthew 2 they appear as the wise men of the East.

30.8 Amen, Aries, the Ram H.D. was deeply immersed in astrology. **Aries,** which in Latin means "the ram," is a constellation containing the stars of the spring equinox, and is the first sign of the Zodiac. Early mythologies identify **the Ram** with Zeus and with Amon/Ammon, the ram God of Egypt. **Aries** is also connected to the Golden Fleece, who bore the mistreated children of King Athamas away. In the Old Testament, Abraham found the ram in the bush and sacrificed him instead of his son Isaac. Typologically, this ram is linked to the later Lamb of

God, the Christ, sacrificed for the world. H.D. connects Amen-Ra, **Amen,** and **Aries the Ram.**

33.4 **Sirius, Vega, Arcturus** **Sirius** or the Dog star is the brightest star in the sky and is located in the constellation canis major. **Vega** is the brightest star in the constellation Lyra. "Vega" in Arabic means "falling eagle." **Arcturus,** from the Greek, meaning "Protector of the Bear," is a giant star, the fourth brightest in the sky. See 121.6.

33.18 **unguent, myrrh, incense** The three wise men or magi stop at Mary's house over which the great star in the sky stops. They bring gifts of gold, incense, and myrrh to the child Jesus. Matthew 2.7–11.

33.19 **jasper, beryl, sapphire** In Revelation, in a vision of the New Jerusalem, the walls of heaven are made of jasper, beryl, and sapphire. Rev. 21.18.

35.5–6 **the phoenix, / your bennu bird** A bird that burns itself up, then rises from its own ashes, and is a symbol of immortality. In Egyptian symbolism, the Phoenix represents the sun dying each night and resurrecting each morning. In Pompeii, where Isis was worshiped, Osiris is depicted in a painting with his **bennu bird.** The bird's head is adorned with Isis's emblems: the uraeus, solar disk, and lunar crescent. See note 4.7.

40.1-6 **Scorpion . . . Archer . . . Goat's horns . . . the Waterman** All astrological references. **Scorpion** corresponds to Scorpio; **Archer** to Sagittarius; **Goat's horns** to Capricorn; **the Waterman** to Aquarius. H.D. wrote in a letter, "I wish Aquarius would get born before we perish" (NHP vi).

40.13 **the elixir of life, philosopher's stone** The notion of the philosopher's stone (also called the elixir of life and the grand magistery) is alchemical and may have its origin in Alexandria. The stone was an imaginary substance capable of transmuting base into gold and restoring youth to the old. See 71.1–2.

40.19–20 **sub-conscious ocean where Fish / move two-ways** Probably a reference to Freud and to the god Janus whom H.D. compares to Freud (TF 100, 102). Fish is a symbol for Christ. See notes 5.13, 105.3.

47.10–11 **Hest, / Aset, Isis** See note 5.18.

48.5–7 palette, / point pen or brush . . . papyrus or parchment See notes for 16.1, 17.11, 48.8–12.

48.8–12 Thoth . . . Hermes-thrice-great . . . his tau-cross H.D. wrote: "Hermes of the Greeks . . . took the attribute of Thoth of the Egyptians. The *T* or Tau-cross became caduceus with twined serpents, again corresponding to the *T* or Tay-cross that Moses lifted from the desert" (TF 101). The Tau-cross, a cross with a loop at the top, also known as an ankh, is an Egyptian symbol of life, fertility, specifically the sun fertilizing the earth. The Egyptian Christians, the Coptics, appropriated the ankh as a symbol of the life-giving power of the Christ's cross. See Caduceus 7.5.

48.15–20 let him (Wisdom) . . . be ye wise / as asps, scorpions, as serpents. H.D. associates the serpent with "the Tree of the knowledge of Good and Evil" as well as with "that serpent of Wisdom that crouched at the feet of the goddess Athené and was one of her attributes, like the spear . . . she held in her hand" (TF 89). H.D. also associates Thoth and Mercury with Athené (TF 52). Athené is the Greek goddess of wisdom. **"Be ye wise . . . / as serpents"** is a quotation from Matthew 10.16 in which Jesus says "Behold, I send you forth as sheep in the midst of wolves: be ye therefore wise as serpents, and harmless as doves." See notes 7.1, 7.5.

49.1–3 the pillar-of-fire When H.D. says the pillar-of-fire "before" and "after," she evidently refers to its appearance in the Old and New Testaments. Images in the New Testament, especially in Revelation, often have their typological origins in the Old Testament. When the children of Israel escape from Egypt, we read, "And the Lord went before them by day in a pillar of a cloud, to lead them the way; and by night in a pillar of fire, to give them light; to go by day and night" (Ex. 13.21d). In Revelation 10.1–2, John writes: "And I saw another mighty angel come down from heaven clothed with a cloud with a cloud: and a rainbow *was* upon his head, and his face *was* as it were the sun, and his feet were pillars of fire. And he had in his right hand a little book open: and he set his right foot upon the sea, and *his* left *foot* on the earth."

49.7–22 we are each, householder, / each with a treasure; . . . for every scribe / which is instructed, // things new and old. Jesus says: "Therefore every scribe *which is* instructed unto the kingdom of heaven is like unto a man *that is* an householder, which bringeth forth out of his treasure *things* new and old." Matthew 13.52. (For another reference to this chapter of Matthew, see **pearl-of-great-price,** 9.24.)

50.1 Thou shalt have none other gods but me The first of the Ten Commandments, delivered by Moses to the people of Israel (Deuteronomy 5.7).

50.3 Triton The largest and innermost of the eight moons of Neptune. In Greek mythology, Triton was the son of Poseidon; the upper half of his body was human, the lower was like a fish. He blew a conch shell or trumpet.

50.9 Orion or Sirius **Orion** is one of the most easily recognizable constellations in the sky. Orion in Greek mythology was a hunter who raped his betrothed. Her father blinded him, but his vision was restored by the rays of the sun. For **Sirius,** see 33.4.

50.10 the Bear The constellation of the seven brightest stars, Ursa Major, also known as the Big Dipper.

50.12 Algorab, Regulus or Deneb **Algorab** is probably a star. **Regulus** is the brightest star in the constellation Leo; its name is prince in Latin. **Deneb** is the brightest star in the constellation Cygnus.

53.9 butterflies The butterfly in Greek story often symbolizes the soul (Gr., *psyche*). In Christian symbolism, it represents immortality and resurrection.

54.2 Osiris See notes for 5.18 and 25.1–4.

54.13 before Abraham was I am In John 8.58, Jesus says, **before Abraham was, I am,** which is an echo of the passage in Exodus 3.14: "And God said unto Moses, I AM THAT I AM: and he said, Thus shalt thou say unto the children of Israel, I AM hath sent me unto you."

55.1–4 in the beginning, Creator, / Fosterer, Begetter, the Same-Forever / in the papyrus-swamp / in the Judean meadow. The **papyrus-swamp** refers to the Egyptian gods, the **Judean meadow** to the Judeo-Christian God, implying that each religion has its own landscape. **in the beginning** also cannot but recall both the first words of Genesis and the Gospel of John. See 17.15–16.

56.15–18 where heat breaks and cracks . . . white, little flowers H.D. explained that the **white little flowers** symbolize life after death: "The mystery of death, first and last—stressed in XL, XLI, XLII, Osiris being the spirit of the underworld, the sun under the world, the setting-sun, the end—implicit there always the idea of the sun-rise—and above all the everlasting miracle of the breath of life—where heat breaks and cracks / the sand-waste / you are a mist / of snow: white, little flowers" (NHP vii).

TRIBUTE TO THE ANGELS

63.1 Hermes Trismegistus See 16.1.

63.10 Mithra's tomb Mithra, a major god of Persia and India (Mitra), was originally a minor god of the Zoroastrians. By the 5th century B.C. the god of light and sun had become the principle Persian god, and dualistic Mithraism was a widespread religion—reaching to Rome. There, through the first two centuries A.D. it had more adherents than Christianity, with which it shared many characteristics including dualism, continence, fasting, and a belief in the immortality of the soul.

64.2 your walls are made of jasper In Rev. 21.18 "the walls of it was *of* jasper" in the city of heaven.

64.3 but not four-square, I thought "The city lieth foursquare." Rev. 21.16.

64.7 twelve foundations "And the wall of the city had twelve foundations, and in them the twelve names of the twelve Apostles of the Lamb." Rev. 14.

64.8 transparent glass Rev. 21.21 describes the street of the city of Heaven: "and the street of the city *was* pure gold, as it were transparent glass."

64.9–10 for no need of the sun / nor moon to shine In God's heavenly city there is no need of sun or moon since the glory of God provides light and the Lamb is the light: "And I saw no temple therein: for the Lord God Almighty and the Lamb are the temple of it. And the city had no need of the sun, neither of moon, to shine in it; for the glory of God did lighten it, and the Lamb *is* the light thereof" (Rev. 21.22–23).

65.1 I John saw "And I John saw these things, and heard *them.*" Rev. 22.8.

65.1–3 I testify; / if any man shall add // God shall add unto him the plagues H.D. condenses Rev. 22.18: "For I testify unto every man that heareth the words of prophecy of this book, If any man shall add unto these things, God shall add unto him the plagues that are written in this book."

65.4–5 but he that sat upon the throne said, / I make all things new. "And he that say upon the throne said, Behold, I make all things new." Rev. 21.5. See 103.9–12.

65.8 He of the seven stars In Revelation, Jesus explains to John the significance of John's vision of the Son of man, who stands in the midst of seven golden candlesticks, holding seven stars in his right hand. "The mystery of the seven stars which thou sawest in my right hand, and the seven golden candlesticks. The seven stars are the seven angels of the seven churches: and seven candlesticks which thou sawest are the seven churches" (Rev. 1.20). Norman Holmes Pearson writes: "*Tribute to the Angels* gives thanks for the services of the seven angels at the throne of God, un-named by Saint John and to-be-named by scribes later, like H.D. herself. Both her book and Saint John's are filled with cited sevens. Even the 43 sections of each third of H.D,'s *Trilogy* add up to seven" (NHP x).

65.9 he of the seventy-times-seven "Then came Peter to him, and said, Lord, how often shall my brother sin against me, and I forgive him? Till seven times? Jesus saith unto him, I say not unto thee, Until seven times: but, Until seventy times seven." Mt. 18.21–22.

66.2 the plowshare for the sword "And he shall judge among the nations, and shall rebuke many people: and they shall beat their swords into plowshares, and their spears into pruning hooks: nation shall not lift up sword against nation, neither shall they learn war any more." (Isaiah 2.4). Similar passages appears in Joel 3.10; Micah 4.3.

66.6 no grape-leaf for the thorn Christ the lamb of God is often depicted standing between grapes and thorns. Jesus says, "Ye shall know them by their fruit. Do men gather grapes of thorns, or figs of thistles." Mt. 7–16.

66.9–10 the voice to quell the re-gathering, / thundering storm H.D. said of *Tribute to the Angels* (which she wrote in a bus): "I really DID feel that a new heaven and a new earth were about to materialize.

It lasted . . . for a few weeks—then D-Day! And the 're-gathering thundering storm'" (NHP ix).

67.1 peace be still Jesus and his followers are on a ship in a storm. They wake him saying, "Master, carest thou not that we perish? And he arose and rebuked the wind and said unto the sea, Peace, be still. And the wind ceased, and there was a great calm. And he said unto them Why are ye so fearful? how is it that ye have no faith?" (Mk 4.39).

67.2 Azrael In the Koran, **Azrael** is the angel who parts the body from the soul at death, whose name in Hebrew means help of God. The name and concept were borrowed from Judaism. H.D. wrote: "The Angel names are more or less traditional O[ld] T[estament], though I use the Mohammedan name for planet Saturn, ruler of time and death, Azrael" (NHP ix).

67.6 Raphael An archangel mentioned in the Apocrypha in the book of Tobit. He is the angel associated with healing, whose name in Hebrew means "God hath healed."

67.6 lovest thou me? After Jesus rose from the dead, he showed himself to his disciples, and tested Peter's faith, asking him three times, lovest thou me? John 21.15, 16, 17.

67.10 Gabriel The messenger archangel who is the herald of good news in Daniel 8.16 and Luke 1.26. In the Annunciation, he told the Virgin Mary she would bear the Son of God, and is often depicted with a lily (symbol of the Virgin). He is also depicted with a trumpet raised.

67.16 Uriel An archangel whose name in Hebrew means light of God.

68.4 Thebes See 3.5.

68.8–9 the battle of the Titans, / saw Zeus' thunderbolts in action In the Greek religion, the Titans were the twelve deities who preceded the Olympian deities before the Olympians overthrew them. Zeus cut off the testicles of his father, Kronos; they fell into the sea off Paphos, Cyprus, and Aphrodite was born in their foam. The name Aphrodite means in Greek "foam-born." Zeus sent Kronos to rule the Island of the Blest (see 120.4–5), and Atlas, a descendant of the Titans, was condemned to carry the sky on his shoulders.

69.3–8 was part of that same fire / that in a candle on a candle-stick // or in a star, / is known as one of seven, // is named among the seven Angels, / Uriel. See 65.8.

70.7–8 purple as with purple spread / upon an atlar The Lord is speaking to Moses and Aaron: "And they shall take away the ashes from the altar, and spread a purple cloth thereon." Num. 4.13.

70.9–10 This is the flowering of the rood, / The flowering of the reed **Rood,** derived from rod, means the cross of Christ (made up of two rods). **Reed** suggests the Reed Sea (the correct name for the Red Sea, which parted for Moses). Rood is related to the New Testament; reed to the Old. See 7.1 and 7.5 and note for the title *The Flowering of the Rod* 111.

71.1–3 Now polish the crucible // and in the bowl distill // a word The reference is to alchemy, the precursor of modern chemistry, whose purpose was to transform base metals into silver and gold. According to legend, it was founded by Thoth, Hermes, the fallen angels, or was revealed by God to Moses and Aaron. Alchemy took on a mystical and magical character. The philosophy of the Hellenistic Greeks of Alexandria was influenced by alchemy, for the conversion of the ordinary into gold was seen as the striving for perfection and sublimation. See 40.3.

71.9 marah-mar Bitter sea. **Marah** is bitter (Hebrew) and **mar** is sea in Spanish.

71.12 mer, mere, mère, mater, Maia, Mary **mer** is sea (Fr.), **mere** is a small lake, pond, or marsh, **mère** is mother (Fr.), **mater** is mother (Lat.), **Maia** is, in Greek mythology, the eldest of the Pleiades and Hermes' mother by Zeus. **Mary** is Mary mother of Jesus, Mary Magdalene, and the other Marys in the New Testament who attend Jesus. See 135.9–10.

73.7 Hesperus The name for the evening star, which is Venus. The planet Venus is brighter than any celestial body, except the sun and the moon.

73.10 Venus, Aphrodite, Astarte **Venus** is Roman goddess of love, **Aphrodite** is Greek goddess of love, **Astarte** is Phoenician goddess of love. See 5.18.

73.13 Phosphorus The name for the morning star, which is also the planet Venus.

74.10–12 mandrake . . . mandragora The Latin name is *Mandragora offincinarum,* a plant in the potato family that resembles the human form, purported to be an aphrodisiac and fertilizer. When it is pulled up, the plant is said to scream and to drive people crazy or kill them. The Greeks associated it with Aphrodite and called its fruit "love apples."

78.1 Annael H.D. wrote: "The Venus name, I believe is Anael but I spelt it ANNAEL; it didn't seem to 'work' until I did—it links on too with Anna, Hannah or Grace, so has an authentic old-testament ring" (NHP ix).

79.11–12 seven, / names among the seven Angels See 65.8.

80.3–4 two of the seven Spirits / set before God John referring to seven churches which are in Asia: "Grace *be* unto you, and peace from him which is, and which was, and which is to come; and from the seven Spirits which are before his throne." Rev. 1.4. (See Rev 3.1, 4.5, 5.6.)

81.9 Thebes and Tyre For **Thebes,** see note 3.5. **Tyre** is a Phoenician city south of present day Beirut, built on a peninsula. It is one of the great cities of ancient days and frequently mentioned in the Bible.

82.3 Astoroth Astarte or Ashtoreth. See note 5.18.

82.14 may-tree or apple **May-tree** is hawthorn, out of which Christ's crown of thorns was made. The **apple** is associated with fruitfulness, immortality, temptation, and magic. The apple and apple tree are associated with the exceedingly good, the best, as in the expression, "the apple of my eye"; and in the Song of Solomon 2.3, they have an erotic dimension: "As the apple tree among trees of the wood, so *is* my beloved among sons. I sat down under his shadow with great delight, and his fruit was sweet to my taste." See note 120.4–5.

87.2 transubstantiation The transubstantiation or the Eucharist (Gr., Thanksgiving) or communion is the Christian sacrament in which the worshiper eats the body of Christ, symbolized by bread, and drinks his blood, symbolized by wine. Catholic doctrine holds that the substances of bread and wine turn miraculously into the substance of Christ. It is based on the story of the Last Supper. See Mt. 26.26–28; Mk. 14.22–24; Lk. 22.19–20.

87.11 the Angel which redeemed me Jacob (who wrestled with the angel) is dying and says to his sons: "The Angel which redeemed me from all evil, bless the lads; and let my name be named on them, and the name of my fathers Abraham and Isaac; and let them grow into a multitude in the midst of the earth" (Gen. 48.16). Jacob's name was changed to Israel. He blesses his twelve sons, whose offspring became the twelve tribes of Israel, and from which the notion of the *twelve* apostles is derived.

87.15–16 This is the flowering of the rood, / this is the flowering of the wood See note 70.9–10.

89.1–2 no need / of the moon to shine in it See note 64.9–10.

91.7–8 be not forgetful / for some have entertained angels unawares. "Let brotherly love continue. Be not forgetful to entertain strangers: for thereby some have entertained angels unawares" (Hebrews 13.1–2). In *The Odyssey* Telemachus encounters the goddess Athena, unaware who she is, but greets her with the courtesy due a stranger at the door: "Greetings stranger! Welcome to our feast." *Odyssey* 1.94.

93.3–6 Our Lady of the Goldfinch, / Our Lady of the Candelabra, // Our Lady of the Pomegranate, / Our Lady of the Chair The **Goldfinch** is associated with fruitfulness, gallantry, and the passion of Christ. There may also be an allusion here to the Salem witch trials. If a yellow bird flew to the hand of an accused, then she was deemed a witch. The Moravians, like the Salem Puritan women, were also persecuted for being heretics and witches. The **Candelabra** may refer to the candlesticks in the Revelation surrounding Christ (and which were probably a Menorah); H.D. puts the Lady at the center, rather than Christ. (See note 65.8.) The **pomegranate** is associated with the fertility of the Great Goddess and of the Virgin Mary; when Hera and Persephone are depicted holding a pomegranate, it symbolizes death and resurrection. Perhaps the **Chair** refers to the chair of justice or to a throne. See H.D.'s *Tribute to Freud* (36–38) for a discussion of her dream of the Lady.

94.4 Levant The collective name for the states of the eastern Mediterranean, from Egypt to Turkey.

94.6 the city of Constantine Constantinople was founded by Constantine I. The former capital of the Byzantine Empire and the Ottoman Empire has been officially called Istanbul since 1930. It was the greatest city in Europe in the Middle Ages. The church of Hagia

Sophia (or Santa Sophia) is in Constantinople. Hagia Sophia is the masterpiece of Byzantine architecture. When the Turks conquered Constantinople, Hagia Sophia was converted to a mosque. The Muslim Turks plastered over the mosaics of Christian figures, including Santa Sophia, and obliterated the Christian symbols. Now many of the mosaics have been restored. See 101.1–2.

96.8 Santa Maria dei Miracoli Saint Mary of the Miracles (It.).

96.11 Maria von dem Schnee Mary of the Snow (Germ.).

97.2–4 white as snow // so as no fuller on earth / can white them. "And his raiment become shining, exceedingly white as snow; so as no fuller on earth can white them" (Mark 9.3). H.D. is describing the Lady with the words used in Revelation for the description of Jesus Christ and in Mark to describe His Transfiguration. See also, "*His* head and *his* hairs *were* white like wool, as white as snow" Rev. 1.14. Also see note 113.2.

97.6–8 clothed with a garment // down to the foot . . . girt about with a golden girdle "And in the midst of the seven candlesticks *one* like unto the Son of man, clothed with a garment down to the foot, and girt about the paps with a golden girdle." Rev. 1.13.

98.1–6 Hermes . . . Thoth . . . T-cross . . . caduceus . . . Hermes Trismegistus See notes 7.1, 7.5, 16.1, 48.8–12.

98.5 Saint Michael A guardian archangel who in Christian tradition is the angel with a sword.

101.1–2 this is Holy Wisdom, / Santa Sophia, the SS of the Sanctus Spiritus 101.4 Holy Ghost 101.7 the fruit of the Tree 101.8 Eve H.D. wrote: "The Latin in the last [part of *Tribute to The Angels*], *vas spirituale / rosa mystica*—are from the Laurentian Litany to the Virgin, R[oman] C[atholic] missal. I think [our friend] is wrong to say there is R.C. implication—I distinctly link the LADY up with Venus-Annael, with the Moon, with the pre-Christian Roman Bona Dea, with the Byzantine Greek church Santa Sophia and the SS of the Sanctus Spiritus" (NHP x). Count Zinzendorf, the founder of the Moravian Church in which H.D. was raised, was denounced as a heretic for claiming that the human soul was female, *anima,* rather than *animus,* and connecting the soul with **Sophia,** the female Holy Spirit of Gnosticism. In her vision seen on her room wall in a Corfu hotel, which she calls the writing-on-the-wall, H.D. saw: "The *S* or half-*S* face the angel; that is, the series of the *S*-pattern opens out in the direction of the angel; they are like question marks . . . this inverted *S*-pattern may have represented a series of question marks, the questions that have been asked through the ages, that the ages will go on asking" (TF 55). In her Gnostic quest for knowledge, she also links the S to the serpent. In Gnosticism the serpent is holy because it represents knowledge, and **Eve** is a savior because she gave knowledge, **the fruit of the Tree,** to humanity. The SS is not a sanctifying of the Nazi SS or the Swastika—H.D. actively opposed the Nazis—but a way of reclaiming her "spiritual realism" (see p. 48).

101.12 she brings the Book of Life, obviously. In the Revelation the names written in the book of life are seen as proof of the doctrine of election: "And I saw the dead, small and great, stand before God; and the books were opened: and another book was opened, which is *the book* of life: and the dead were judged out of those things which were written in the books, according to their works. . . . And death and hell were cast into the lake of fire. This is the second death. And whosoever was not found written in the book of life was cast into the lake of fire" (20.12–15). In describing God's heavenly city, John writes: "And all that dwell upon the earth shall worship him, whose names are not written in the book of life of the Lamb slain from the foundation of the world" (13.8). He also writes: "And there shall in no wise enter into it any thing that defileth, neither *whatsoever* worketh abomination, no *maketh* a lie: but they which are written in the Lamb's book of life" (21.27). H.D. quotes from chapter 21 of Revelation, which decribes "the holy city, new Jerusalem" (21.2) throughout *Tribute to the Angels.*

102.5 Corinthian capitals The temple at Corinth was devoted to Aphrodite.

102.6 Coptic nave The Coptics are Egyptian Christians.

103.5–6 She is the Vestal / from the days of Numa Vesta is the goddess of the hearth, identified with the Greek goddess Hestia, whose temple contains a sacred fire tended by the vestal virgins. Numa Pompilius was a legendary king of Rome. He began these ceremonial and religious rites, including those of the vestal virgins.

103.8 Bona Dea An ancient fertility goddess worshiped only by women. No man could be present at her festival, which was held in May. Bona Dea means "good goddess" (Lat.).

103.9–12 She carries a book but it is not / the tome of the ancient wisdom, // the pages, I imagine, are the blank pages of the unwritten volume of the new Ezra Pound coined the famous exhortation to modernist writers "make it new." In Revelation, John is instructed by God: "And he that sat upon the throne said, Behold, I make all things new. And he said unto me, write: for these words are true and faithful" Rev. 21.5. (See 65.4–5.) H.D.'s vision in which the "new Eve" or the Lady carries "the Book of Life" creates a contrast between her revelation and John's. In John's Revelation the text of the book is eternal and unchangable; in H.D.'s version the book has blank pages for new writers. See 65.1–3, 101.12.

103.16 Sibyl There were several sibyls who had prophetic power. Apollo offered the Sibyl of Cumae anything she liked if she would become his lover. She asked to live as many years as the grains of dust contained in a pile of sweepings, but forgot to ask him for perpetual youth. She became so old and shriveled that she hung in a cave upside-down in a bottle. When children asked her what she wanted, she answered, "I want to die." T.S. Eliot began *The Waste Land* (1922) with a epigraph that ends with the Sibyl's words, "I want to die."

103.19 Psyche, the butterfly See note 53.9

105.3 a tale of a Fisherman "Now as he walked by the sea of Galilee, he saw Simon and Andrew his brother casting a net into the sea: for they were fishers. And Jesus said unto them, Come ye after me, and I will make you to become fishers of men." Mk. 1.16–17. See also Mt. 4.18–19. See 40.19–20.

105.4 a tale of a jar or jars In *The Flowering of the Rod,* H.D. refers to the biblical alabaster "box" as a "jar." See 129.12 and 143.13–14.

107.15–16 no need of the moon to shine . . . / I saw no temple. See 64.9–10.

108.2 Zadkiel H.D. wrote: "Old Zadkiel is really our old Amen again—now having an angel-name; there is a traditional Zadkiel but do not know if mentioned in Writ—but there is Uriel, I believe, and some are named in the Aprocryphal *Book of Enoch* which I can never place" (NHP x).

108.3 Jupiter The Roman father of the gods. In Greek he is Zeus.

108.4 Zeus-pater or Theus-pater **Zeus** in ancient Greek religion is the great father-god. **Theus** is god (Gr.); **pater** is father (Lat.).

109.11 I John saw. I testify See 65.1, 65.1–3.

109.14 jasper See 33.19.

109.19 vas spirituale Spiritual vessel. See 101.1–2.

109.20 rosa mystica Mystical rose. See 101.1–2.

THE FLOWERING OF THE ROD

111 The Flowering of the Rod Refers to: the Caduseus of Hermes, Thoth, Mercury; the flowering of Aaron's rod in the Old Testament, symbolizing authority over rebellious tribes who would turn to worshiping Baal; and the flowering of the cross of rods (roods) in the New Testament, symbolizing the resurrection of Jesus. See 7.1, 7.5, 70.9–10.

113.2 the beautiful raiment Reference to the Transfiguration: "And after six days Jesus taketh *with him* Peter, and James, and John, and leadeth them up into an high mountain apart by themselves: and he was transfigured before them. And his raiment became shining, exceeding white as snow; so as no fuller on earth can white them" (Mark 9.2–3). To show that Jesus is His Son, God speaks: "and a voice out of the cloud, saying, This is my beloved Son: hear him." Mk. 9.7. See Mt. 17.1–8, Lk. 9.28–36. See 97.2–4.

113.8 Hermon One of the mountains in the Song of Solomon 4.8. Also the place of the Transfiguration, according to H.D. (though this is not probable). H.D. seems to be juxtaposing the Song of Solomon with the Transfiguration. See 160.1–2.

113.16 the terrible banner "Thou *art* beautiful, O my love, as Tirzah, comely as Jerusalem, terrible as *an army* with banners." Song of Solomon 6.4. See also Song of Solomon 6.10.

115.17 The-place-of-the-skull Golgatha, which in Hebrew means the place of the skull, is where Jesus was crucified. Golgotha is also called Calvary, from the Latin *Calvaria,* meaning skull.

116.9 wild-goose The goose is sacred to Isis, Osirus-Thoth, and to Aphrodite as a symbol of love.

117.2 Atlantis In Greek legend, a wondrously beautiful island in the Atlantic ocean, which Plato describes as a utopia in his dialogues *Timaeus* and *Critias.* This ideal state was destroyed by an earthquake. It is now believed that the island Thira (Santorini), with its great Bronze-Age civilization, may have been Atlantis. In the 13th century B.C., two-thirds of the island caved into the sea when a volcano erupted.

117.5–6 to-day shalt thou be / with me in Paradise From Luke 23.43. Jesus is on the cross speaking to one of the criminals, also crucified, who defended him against the taunts of the other criminal.

120.4–6 Hesperides . . . golden apple-trees The **Hesperides** were maidens who, along with a dragon or serpent, guarded the tree with the golden apples in a fabulous garden at the western edge of the world, on the Blessed Island of the Dead. The tree is also called the Tree of Life. See 128.8–9.

121.6 Arcturus The fourth brightest star in the sky. When it rises at night it announces spring, when it rises at dawn, it announces the harvest. See 33.4.

122.7 Islands of the Blest See 120.4–6.

122.8 many waters can not quench love's fire "Many waters cannot quench love, neither can the floods down it: if a man would give all the substance of his house for love, it would be utterly contemned." Song of Solomon 8.7.

124.4 full of new wine In Acts, people speak in tongues in praise of God's deeds. Some who hear are amazed that they speak in so many languages, while "others mocking said, These men are full of new wine" (Acts 2.13). Peter says that they are not drunk but acting according to the prophesy of Joel in which people will prophesy, see visions, and dream.

124.10–14 iron, steel, metal . . . into the Golden Age In *Works and Days,* by the Greek poet Hesiod (8th century B.C.), there are five ages of humans: the Golden Age, Silver Age, Bronze Age, Heroic Age, and Iron Age. The Golden Age ruled by Kronos is a period of peace and eternal spring.

126.5–6 from a frozen Priestess, / a lonely Pythoness The Pythoness is the Pythian. See 4.3

126.15 lily See 7.3.

127.5–12 the least of all seeds . . . it is the greatest among herbs / and becometh a tree In the parable of the mustard seed, Jesus says, "The kingdom of heaven is like to a grain of mustard seed, which a man took, and sowed in his field: Which indeed is the least of all seeds: but when it is grown, it is the greatest among herbs, and becometh a tree, so that the birds of the air come and lodge in the branches thereof" (Lk. 13.31–32). See also Mk. 4.31, Mt. 13.31.

128.7–9 He was the first to wing / from that sad Tree // but having flown, the Tree of Life The sad Tree is the cross; the Tree of Life stood in the Garden of Eden next to the Tree of the Knowledge of Good and Evil. See 120.4–5.

128.18 to-day shalt thou be / with me in Paradise See 117.5–6.

129.7–9 who was naturally reviled for having left home / and not caring for housework . . . or was that / Mary of Bethany? // in any case—as to this other Mary In Luke, Martha receives Jesus in her home, and is upset that her sister Mary cares more for hearing the Lord's word that for doing housework. When Martha asks Jesus to tell Mary to help her, Jesus replies: "Martha, Martha, thou art careful and troubled about many things: But one thing is needful: And Mary hath chosen that good part, which shall not be taken away from her" (Lk. 10.41–42). At the tomb of Jesus: "And there was Mary Magdalene and this other Mary, sitting over against the sepulchre." Mt. 27.61. See 135. 9–10.

129.12 the alabaster jar H.D. calls the biblical alabaster box a "jar." See Luke 7.37, Mk. 14.3, and Mt. 26.7. See 143.13–14.

129.16 neither purse nor script Jesus is instructing seventy new followers: "Carry neither purse, nor script, nor shoes: and salute no man by the way. And into whatever house ye enter, first say, Peace *be* to this house." Lk.10.4–5.

129.17–18 no gold-piece or silver / stamped with the image of Caesar Jesus asks those who bring him a penny, "Whose *is* this image and superscription? And they said unto him, Caesar's. And Jesus answering said unto them, Render to Caesar the things that are Caesar's, and to God the things that are God's" (Mk. 12.16–17). See Mt. 22.21–22, Lk. 20.24–25.

132.14 the Princesses of the Hyksos Kings The Hyksos were a Semitic people who conquered Egypt between 1720–1710 B.C. and who subdued the pharaohs of the Middle Kingdom. They introduced Canaanite deities into Egypt.

135.9–10 I am Mary—O, there are Marys a-plenty, / (though I am Mara, bitter) I shall be Mary-myrrh For **Mara,** see 71.9, 71.12. For **Mary-myrrh,** see 10.17–18, 33.8, 135.16, 143.13–14. The name Mary is Maria or Mariam in the New Testament, the Greek form of the Hebrew Miriam. The name may be derived from the Egyptian Maryē, meaning "Beloved." There are several Marys in the New Testament (**Marys a-plenty**). Mary is the mother of Jesus. Mary of Bethany is the sister of Martha and Lazarus, and John claims it was this Mary that anointed Jesus: "(It was *that* Mary which anointed the Lord with ointment, and wiped his feet with her hair, whose brother Lazarus was sick)" Jn.11.2. All four Gospels have an account of a woman anointing Jesus (Mt. 26.6–13, Mk. 14.3–9, Lk. 7.37–50, Jn. 12.1–8), but it is not clear whether they are referring to the same woman. The sinful woman in Luke 7 has been identified as Mary Magdalene, though Luke does not name her. Jesus casts out seven devils from Mary Magdalene in Mk. 16.9, Lk. 8.2. Mary Magdalene appears at the crucifixion with Mary the mother of James and Joses. When the women arrive at the tomb they "had brought sweet spices, that they might come and anoint him" (Lk. 16.1). Another Mary appears when Peter escapes from prison: "he came to the house of Mary, the mother of John, whose surname was Mark; where many were gathered together praying" (Acts 12.12). There is also a Mary who is greeted by St. Paul in Rom. 16.

135.16 Attis-Adonis-Tammuz and his mother who was myrrh. In the Phrygian religion Attis was a vegetation god, and like Adonis he was worshiped as a vegetation god of resurrection, responsible for birth, death, and rebirth of plant life. By the time of his adoption by the Romans, he was celebrated as a powerful celestial god of spring resurrection. Adonis (meaning lord, like Hebrew Adonai) was the son of Myrrha. (See 10.18.) He was beautiful and also worshiped as a vegetation god. Aphrodite and Persephone were in love with him and struggled over him. After he was gored to death by a boar, Zeus solved the dispute by having him spend half the year (spring and summer months) above ground with Aphrodite and half the year underground with Persephone. Tammuz, a Babylonian god of agriculture and flocks, personified spring resurrection. The fertility goddess Ishtar loved him and when he died journeyed to the underworld to bring him back. In another legend, she killed him and restored him to life. His death and rebirth correspond to the festivals of Adonis and Attis.

139.7 a Chaldean Chaldea is in the southernmost valley of the Tigris and the Euphrates rivers. The Chaldeans entered Babylonia in about 1000 B.C. Because astronomy and astrology were developed during their rule, "Chaldean" came to mean astrologer.

139.9 Balthasar, Melchior Two of the Wise Men, Magi, or Three Kings. Caspar (or Kaspar) is the third.

140.5 Abraham Abraham of Ur, descendent of Adam and Shem, was the father of the Jews. He made the earliest covenant with God, and brought his people into Canaan.

141.2 the house was filled with odour of the ointment In John's version of the story of Mary washing Jesus's feet: "Then took Mary a pound of spikenard, very costly, and anointed the feet of Jesus, and wiped his feet with her hair: the house was filled with the odour of the ointment" (John 12.3). See 159.10.

141.14–15 Judas whispered to his neighbour / and then they all began talking about the poor In John's version Judas Iscariot criticizes Mary's anointing of Jesus's feet. "Then saith one of his disciples, Judas Iscariot, Simon's *son,* which should betray him, Why was not this ointment given to the poor?" John 12.4–5.

142.1 Simon See 146.2–7.

142.10–13 Siren, Mermaid, Siren-song Emphasizing the erotic dangers of the anointment in the next lines, Simon connects Mary's hair with a **Siren** and a fatal **Siren-song.** In *The Odyssey,* the Sirens with their seductive singing cause shipwrecks and drowning. Odysseus strapped himself to his mast so he could hear the beautiful allure of their song without being free to yield to temptation. A mermaid has the same characteristics as a siren.

143.13–14. this man if he were a prophet, would have known / who and what manner of woman this is. The story of a woman washing the feet of Jesus with her tears, drying them with her hair, kissing and anointing them with myrrh, appears in each of the gospels, with variations. "And, behold, a woman in the city, which was a sinner, when she knew that *Jesus* sat at meat in the Pharisee's house, brought an alabaster box of ointment, and stood at his feet behind *him* weeping, and began to wash his face, and did wipe *them,* with the hairs of her head, and kissed his feet, and anointed *them* with the ointment. Now when the Pharisee which had bidden saw *it* [the woman's washing the feet of Jesus], he spake within himself, This man if he were a prophet, would have known who and what manner of woman this is that toucheth him: for she is a sinner" (Luk. 7.37–39). Christ says to Simon: "Seest thou this woman? I entered into thine house, thou gavest me no water for my feet; but she hath washed my feet with tears, and wiped *them* with the hairs of her head. Thou gavest me no kiss: but this woman since the time I came in hath not ceased to kiss my feet. My head with oil thou didst not anoint: but this woman hath anointed my feet with ointment. Wherefore I say unto thee, Her sins which are many are forgiven; for she loved much; but to whom little is forgiven *the same* loveth little. And he said unto her, thy sins are forgiven" (Luke. 7.44–48). See 135.9–10.

144.1–4 Balthasar . . . Melchior . . . Gaspar or Kaspar See 139.9.

145.15 Isis, Astarte, Cyprus Aphrodite was born in the sea off Paphos, Cyprus. See note 5.18.

145.18–20 Ge-meter, De-meter, earth-mother // or Venus / in a star In Greek Ge is earth; metron is measure, hence, measure of the earth, as in geometer. It is also a pun on **De-meter,** which is thought to mean earth-mother (De or da probably means earth; meter means mother). In this word, invented by H.D., is also Ge (Gaia) the earth goddess, born of Chaos and one of the first heavenly beings. Ge's children were Uranus, the sky, and Pontus, the sea. As an earth goddess she was also an underworld deity, and ruled over an oracular center at Delphi (under which was the world's navel, the pit) and another center in Olympia. In Rome she was Tellus or Terra. **Demeter,** in Greek religion, is the goddess of fertility and harvest. When her daughter Persephone was abducted she grieved so much the earth became barren. Searching for her daughter, she went to Eleusis, where the Eleusinian mysteries were initiated in her honor. The Thesmophoria, a fertility festival also in her honor, was attended only by women. The **earth-mother** was common to religions all over the earth. See Ge or Gaia above. **Venus in a**

star. Although Venus is called the evening and morning star, it is a planet.

146.2–7 Simon Peter . . . Simon of Cyrene . . . Simon the sorcerer . . . the leper **Simon Peter** is the disciple and apostle of Jesus and brother of Andrew. Jesus gave him the name Peter (Gr., *Petros,* Heb./Aramaic, *Kepha*), meaning stone. **Simon of Cyrene** was a Jew probably from the Greek port city of Cyrene in present-day Libya. On the way to Golgotha where Jesus was crucified, the soldiers pressed Simon of Cyrene into carrying Jesus's cross, according to Mt. 27.32 and Mk. 15.6. But John disagrees. In John 19.17, Jesus carries his own cross to Golgotha. **Simon the sorcerer** of Samaria is Simon Magus, a heretic of the second century, who attempts in Acts 8.9–25 to buy powers from the apostles with his silver, hence, the sin of *simony.* He is baptized and coverted by Peter. Simon of the Acts is most certainly confused with the more famous Simon the sorcerer, who is Simon Magus, the early heretic most hated by the church fathers, and who founded one of the first Gnostic sects. He held himself to be the savior, was a flamboyant magician, and in the extracanonical Acts of Peter has a daring contest with Peter in the Roman forum where he flies over Rome. In the house of **Simon the leper,** Jesus's hair was anointed by Mary. Mt. 13.55. Mk. 6.3. See 143.13–14.

148.15 Jupiter Jupiter is the largest planet in the solar system. See 108.3–4.

149.3–5 in her were forgiven / the sins of the seven / daemons cast out of her "Now when *Jesus* was risen early the first *day* of the week, he appeared to Mary Magdalene, out of whom he had cast seven devils." Mk. 16.9. See also Lk. 8.2.

153.13–16 islands of the Blest . . . Hesperides . . . Atlantis See 117.2 and 120.4–6.

157.1–2 Lilith born before Eve / and one born before Lilith Lilith was Adam's first wife and a nocturnal demon lover of Jewish mythology. The word Lilith probably comes from the Assyrian storm demon Lilitu. She also seems to be the earlier "maid of desolation" (*artdat lili*) in the Sumerian Inanna's garden, who was then expelled to become the "demon of waste places." In her biblical incarnation, commentators have designated Lilith to be the "female" in the first creation story: "So God created man in his *own* image, in the image of God created he him; male and *female* created he them" (Gen. 1.27). Here, in contrast to the second creation story (Gen. 2.4), where God in one day creates heaven and earth, Eden, and Adam alone in the garden, God creates both man and woman. Rabbinical Talmudic tradition used Gen. 1.27 ("male and *female* created he them") to show that God created Adam and Lilith simultaneously from the dust. Since they were born equal, at the same time, Lilith will not recognize that Adam is her superior, nor will she be his servant, and she is turned out of Paradise. When she returns to Eden, she sleeps with Adam and has many children who are evil spirits. After another of her expulsions she refuses to return to Adam, and loses one hundred of her offspring each day. In the Muslim tradition, when Lilith returns to Eden, she cohabits with the Devil and gives birth to the jinn. After Lilith's final expulsion, God makes Eve from one of Adam's ribs. In our day, Lilith has been seen as a symbol of woman's unwillingness to assume an inferior station. **one born before Lilith:** It is uncertain who was born before Lilith, since according to legend she and Adam were born at the same time.

159.10 spikenard, very costly See 141.2.

160.1–2 Hermon, the place of the Transfiguation See 113.2 and 113.8.

160.7–8 even Solomon . . . was not arrayed like one of these After the Sermon on the Mount, and the Beatitudes, Jesus tells the multitudes not to worry about the earthly concerns of food, drink and clothing, but to have faith: "Consider the lilies of the field, how they grow; they toil not, neither do they spin: And yet I say unto you, That even Solomon in all his glory was not arrayed like one of these. Wherefore, if God so clothe the grass of the field, which to day is and to morrow is cast into the oven, shall *he,* not much more clothe you, O ye of little faith?" Mt. 6.28–30.

160.9 the almond-trees See note for title *Flowering of the Rod,* 111, also 70.9–10.

160.12 Lebanon Mentioned in the Song of Solomon for Hermon mountain and for its beauty.

161.1 Hebron The highest town in Palestine, 927 meters above sea level. Abraham lived there and bought the field of Machpelah and the cave there as a burial site. Abraham, Sarah, Isaac, Rebekah, Leah, and Jacob were buried there. (Gen. 49.30–33.) In Hebron David was anointed King of Judah, and then King of Israel. (2 Samuel 2.4, 2 Samuel 5.1–3.) Later Absalom rebeled against David, also in Hebron. (2 Samuel 15.)

169.5–6 Bathasar . . . Melchior See 139.9.

Note on deleted sections of *The Flowering of the Rod* In the notes of *H.D.: Collected Poems 1912–1944* (New Directions, 1983, pp. 622–624), editor Louis L. Martz includes four beautiful sections of *The Rod* which H.D. omitted from the book's text. Martz notes: "Among the typescripts [of *Trilogy*] we find the following sections with the heading in H.D.'s hand: 'Dec. 1944. / Deleted from: / The Rod.'"

A NOTE ON H.D.'S LIFE

Hilda Doolittle was born September 10, 1886, in Bethlehem, Pennsylvania, where she spent her childhood in a Moravian community. Her father, Charles Doolittle, was a professor of astronomy at Lehigh University. Her mother, Helen Doolittle was deeply involved in the leadership of the semi-mystical Moravian church and came from a German-Polish family descended from the Unitas Fratrum, a Bohemian brotherhood that left Germany for America in the 1840s to found, among its first three cities, Bethlehem. The Doolittle family were early settlers from England. Uncomfortable with her "quaint" name Hilda Doolittle, she later took Ezra Pound's suggestion to make it simply H.D., which remained her literary name for life. In 1896 when she was ten, the family moved to Philadelphia where her father had accepted a position at the University of Pennsylvania. In Philadelphia, the Quaker meeting house replaced the Moravian church.

In 1901 while still at the Moravian Girls' Seminary, she met Ezra Pound at a Halloween party. A few years later she was at Bryn Mawr College, and Pound, having returned from Hamilton College, was a graduate student at Penn. In 1905, H.D. and Pound were engaged, an incident thoroughly disapproved of by Hilda's parents. H.D. withdrew from Bryn Mawr the next year and studied at home until 1910. By then Pound was off to Venice and London where he, F.S. Flint, T.E. Hulme, Richard Aldington, and others became the literary group known as the Imagists. H.D. settled in London in 1911, studied with Aldington, and soon became central to the group. She published her first Imagist poems under the name "H.D. Imagiste" (the name and label were Pound's). When Pound left her, she married Richard Aldington; the next year Pound married Dorothy Shakespear. Despite later claims by individual Imagists about how slight their involvement was in the movement (except Pound who took credit for inventing it), Imagism did launch a number of young outsider poets onto the London literary scene.

In 1914 H.D. met D.H. Lawrence and Katherine Mansfield. Her friendship with Lawrence was passionate and ended with disappointment and anger, yet both continued to esteem each other until Lawrence's death in 1930. The next years saw H.D. diversely published in anthologies and literary reviews, and in 1916 she published her first book of poems, *Sea Garden*. It appeared in London with Constable & Co. and in Boston and New York with Houghton Mifflin. After Aldington enlisted in the army, H.D. took over for her husband as literary editor of the *Egoist* where she remained until 1917 when she was replaced by T.S. Eliot. The next year her brother Gilbert was killed in France during the Great War.

A major figure entered the poet's life in 1918, Bryher Ellerman. Intelligent, domineering, admiring, and rich, Bryher was to accompany her on trips, eventually live with her for some years, and be a "guardian angel" until H.D.'s death. In 1919 H.D.'s daughter Perdita was born and the same year her husband left her. She sought help from Bryher. Meanwhile, she published her translation of Euripides and more poems. In 1920 she traveled with Bryher to Greece and America, where as author of three books she was warmly received by poets and editors, among them Amy Lowell, Marianne Moore, and Louis Untermeyer. William Carlos Williams came to visit at her hotel, along with his younger friend Robert McAlmon, a novelist. McAlmon and Bryher married some months later in New York "in name" only, so that Bryher could be legally free of her father and McAlmon could receive financial freedom.

Back in London in 1921, H.D. wrote, had friends, and disappointments. She took up partial residence in Switzerland, but continued her extensive travels. In 1923 she went to Egypt with her mother, Bryher, and Perdita, which influenced her deeply, as can be seen in *Trilogy*. She also traveled to Paris, where she was in touch with the *literati* and many expatriates, but she had limited interest in the famous Paris café life. Always prolific, by 1925 she had published three new books, *Hymen* (Egoist/Holt, 1921), *Heliodora and Other Poems* (Jonathan Cape/Houghton Mifflin, 1924), and *Collected Poems of H.D.* (Boni & Liveright, 1925). In 1926 in Paris she published *Palimpsest* (a title true to her work) with Contact Editions, which was run by McAlmon, whom Bryher divorced the next year. Then, also in 1927, Bryher suddenly married Kenneth Macpherson, H.D.'s new lover, in order to provide financial backing to Kenneth so he could continue his alliance with H.D. Macpherson began to make films, and in *Foothills*, H.D. played the main role. Macpherson also started the first film magazine, *Close-Up*, and it was immediately successful. Soon H.D. was connected with the great German film directors G. W. Pabst and Fritz Lang. She wrote and then produced with Macpherson their most important film, *Borderline*, in which she acted opposite the American actor and singer Paul Robeson and momentarily fell in love with him. For H.D., her excursion into films, when the industry was young and experimental, was immensely stimulating. The book version of *Borderline* was published by the Mercury Press in London in 1930. By now she had also put out *Hedylus* (Houghton Mifflin, 1928) to be followed by *Red Roses for Bronze* (Chatto & Windus, London, 1931/Houghton Mifflin, 1931).

The culminating event occurred in 1933 when Sigmund Freud, then seventy-seven, agreed to welcome H.D., forty-seven, as his analysand for a period of one month, at his apartment at 19 Bergasse in Vienna. The following year, 1934, she returned to Vienna to complete her sessions with the master, whom she would celebrate and gently criticize in *Tribute to Freud* (Pantheon, 1956). In the late '30s H.D. was increasingly disturbed by the impending war. She spent much time discussing with Freud what could be done and with Freud and Bryher worked to help rescue and finance Jewish emigration. When the situation deteriorated, Bryher used her financial resources to help Jews flee Germany into Switzerland, and following the Nazi invasion of Austria on March 11, 1938, through Marie Bonaparte, Ernest Jones, and the diplomatic intervention of the American ambassador to France, W. C.

Bullit, among others, the members of the Vienna Psychoanalytical Society were permitted to emigrate to London. In London, the doctor lived in a small apartment on Sloane Street where H.D. visited him. He died in 1939 in Hamstead.

When war broke out, H.D. stayed in London, and during the war period, she and Bryher lived together. Among her many wartime friends were the Sitwells and Norman Holmes Pearson, her admirer at Yale, who would eventually become her assiduous literary agent and executor. Shadowed by the war and England's survival, she published her syncretistic poetic scripture, *The Walls Do Not Fall* in 1944, and in the same year wrote *Tribute to the Angels* and *The Flowering of the Rod.* In 1973, twelve years after her death, they appeared together for the first time in the New Directions book *Trilogy.* When Ezra Pound, her former fiancé and mentor, supported fascism and broadcasted for Mussolini over Rome Radio, H.D.'s relations with him ceased. During his years in St. Elizabeth's Hospital for the Criminally Insane and after his return to Rapallo they corresponded. However, she declined his request to see her in Kusnacht in the last years of her life.

In 1946 H.D. decided to move alone to Lausanne, Switzerland, where she lived in the Hotel de la Paix. There she spent the next six years. She had recovered from depression and electric shock treatment and entered the most prolific years of an already productive life. She published *By Avon River* (Macmillan, 1949), gathered her *Selected Poems,* which Grove put out in 1957, and completed her epic book of "cantos," *Helen in Egypt.* She also finished *End to Torment: A Memoir of Pound* (New Directions, 1973) and her novel based on Richard Aldington, *Bid Me to Live* (Grove Press, 1960).

Then at age sixty-seven, in 1953, H.D. suffered an abdominal occlusion and was operated on in Lausanne. After a second operation, with Bryher's intervention, she moved to a medical residence in Kusnacht, some miles outside Zurich. She was happy in her sanitarium. In 1956 Norman Holmes Pearson managed to lure her back to America for a visit in which she was celebrated at Yale. In 1960 she returned again to America to receive the Gold Medal

Award from the American Academy of Arts and Letters, the first award of its kind and their highest honor. When she returned, she completed *Hermetic Definition,* which contained the lines, "I did not know that I must keep faith / with something, I called it writing / write, write or die." In July, 1961, she had a stroke and died on the 28th of September. The day before her death she received her copy of *Helen in Egypt.* She was buried on Nisky Hill in Bethlehem, Pennsylvania.